The Gospel Octagon

God's Divine Storyline

Parker Foster

Scripture quotations are taken from the King James Version of the Bible.
Edited by Parker Foster and Jeanette Foster
Cover designed by Parker Foster
Copyright © 2015 by P & J Avenue

GospelOctagon@gmail.com.

DEDICATION

The Gospel Octagon is first dedicated to my Creator, Savior, and King, Jesus Christ. He is the One who gave me the idea for this work. Secondly, this book is dedicated to my spectacular wife for all of her assistance in helping me complete this project.

ABOUT THE AUTHOR

The author is a son of the King, Jesus Christ. Years ago the Lord saved him from a lifestyle of sin (1 Tm 1:15). God called him out of darkness and into the light to follow The Lord all the days of his life on this earth, and forever in God's eternal Kingdom. Parker married the love of his life at the age of 29 and they live in Texas. After getting a business degree, he went on to study education at The University of North Texas, Christian Ministry at Wayland Baptist University and Theology at Southwestern Baptist Theological Seminary. He has been a passionate student of the Bible since he became a born-again Christian, with an eagerness to teach others the truths of God's Word. Vocationally, he served in two churches, and two private Christian k-12 schools, where he grew as a teacher and a follower of Christ. Parker's prayer is that this book will explain the biblical Gospel, teach an overview of the Bible, excite you to read your Bible, and through all this bring glory to God alone.

CONTENTS

FORWARD

The Bible is all about the Gospel of Jesus Christ. Yet, if you ask Christians around the world, What is the Gospel? you will likely receive many different answers. Why? Why don't Christians have a simple, straightforward answer to this question? So, how would *you* answer the question, What is the Gospel?

A biblical answer is of upmost importance because The Lord Jesus' last words to His disciples were, *"Go ye into all the world, and preach the Gospel to every creature. He that believeth and is baptized shall be saved; but he that believeth not shall be damned" (Mk 16:15)*. If Christians are to be obedient to our Creator and Savior then we need to know *what the Gospel is* so we can proclaim it to every creature.

A few years ago I read a book that helped me to begin dissecting this question. That book analyzed the apostle's words in five passages of Scripture (1 Co 15:1-4; Ro 1-4; Ac 3:18-19; 10:39-43; 13:38-39). I found *Acts 3* and *Romans 1-4* the most helpful in supporting the author's point, which was that the apostles would share the Gospel by touching on the following four categories:[1]

1. God the Creator
2. Man's Sin
3. Jesus the Savior
4. Man's Response (faith and repentance)

When I began probing this question I had been a passion-
ately committed Christian for eight years, yet, I didn't have a clear
answer for this basic question. After discovering these four points
were the framework of the apostle's Gospel message, I was elated!
Now I had a biblical model to follow as I shared God's good news of
salvation. About two months later I started a Bible study group. Our
study began with answering the question, What is the Gospel? My
heart was excited! I was blessed with the opportunity to equip fellow
believers with the biblical way to share the Gospel. We kickstarted
our study with an overview of the four points. As the study concluded, I was surprised when one person spoke up and disagreed.
He looked at me and said something like, "You are wrong. When we
share the Gospel we only need to talk about Jesus and not sin." Re-
spectfully I responded, "If we go up to an unbeliever and tell them
Jesus is the life, death and the resurrection. He loves you. Believe in
Him and all will be well. That does not make sense to people." I further explained people must first know who Jesus is (the Creator of
the heaven's and the earth). Secondly, all people have sinned and
there are consequences for sin (eternal death). Thirdly, the Creator
God loved people so much He put on flesh, lived a sinless life, died a
sinner's death, and defeated sin and death by rising from the grave.
Lastly, if people are to be saved from their sin, they must respond to
God by repenting (turning from their sin) and putting their faith in
Jesus Christ for the forgiveness of their sin. Sadly, my friend disagreed with me. I was confused. Why didn't he agree? Instead of
walking away feeling like a hero, I left the church that night troubled
and confused. I kept thinking, "people *must* understand they are
stained with sin and there is a serious consequence for their sin before they can be expected to recognize or even desire their need for
the Savior." Unfortunately, my friend did not return to our Bible
study. Over the next four or five months I kept processing the question, What is the Gospel? I began asking myself, Was my friend
right?

Following months of prayer and study, I came to the conclusion there are three biblical answers to this question which I believe every Christian should know. The answers are complimentary and build off each other. Each answer is useful depending on the situation a Christian is in when they are being obedient to the Lord in sharing the Gospel. The three answers are:

1. The Short Answer
2. The Evangelistic Answer
3. The Full Answer

You will encounter a variety of opportunities in your life when one of these three answers fits best. Here is a brief explanation of each.

The Short Answer

The short answer to the question, What is the Gospel? comes from *1 Corinthians* 15:1-4, which says,

> Moreover, brethren, I declare unto you the Gospel which I preached unto you, which also ye have received, and wherein ye stand; By which also ye are saved, if ye keep in memory what I preached unto you, unless ye have believed in vain. **For I delivered unto you first of all that which I also received, how that Christ died for our sins according to the scriptures; And that he was buried, and that he rose again the third day according to the scriptures...**

In this text Paul states the Corinthian believers need to remember the words he taught them. He then gives them a brief overview in verses 3-4. The overview begins with Christ. *Christ* means Savior in the original Greek language. So right off Paul informs his readers that Jesus is a Savior. Well, this begs the question, What does He save you from? Paul and the Corinthians knew Jesus was and is the Savior from sin and sin's consequences. Paul goes on to say that Christ died for our sins according to the Scriptures. Clearly, Paul isn't shying away from talking about sin. He states the reason

Christ died was because of *our sins*. Paul goes on to say Jesus was buried and rose from the grave on the third day.

The short answer to the question, What is the Gospel? is: **Jesus Christ lived, died, and rose again on the third day to defeat the curse caused by sin, and those who believe on Him will be saved from eternal death and inherit eternal life.** Although this answer is biblical, it should be used as a summary of truths already communicated, like Paul did in his letter to the Corinthian *believers*. Paul was not witnessing to unbelievers. The short answer is handy when you are trying to be brief and provide only the most basic overview of the Gospel without going into extensive detail with *fellow believers in Christ*.

The Evangelistic Answer

The evangelistic answer to the question, What is the Gospel? is the format the apostles used or what I also call **the four point Gospel presentation**. Again, the four points are:

1. **God the Creator**
2. **Man's Sin**
3. **Jesus the Savior**
4. **Man's Response** (faith and repentance)

The reason this is called the evangelistic answer is because the word *Gospel* comes from the Greek word *evangelion*,[2] which is where the English word *evangelist* derives from. An evangelist is someone who brings the Gospel, which means good news.[3] These four points are a guide to know what to cover when one is seeking to present the Gospel for witnessing purposes. Each of the points should be elaborated on in detail depending on how much time you have to invest in the conversation. For example, here is a way to present the Gospel utilizing the evangelistic format.

God the Creator

The Bible says in the beginning God created the heavens and the earth. He brought into being the universe, earth, stars, galaxies, plants, animals of all kinds, and finally man and woman. When The Lord was done with His creation He said, *"it was very good" (Gn 1:31)*. He walked with and taught the two people He made, Adam and Eve. They were both extremely intelligent, being made in God's image (Gn 1-2). The world they lived in was perfect, for it was made by God alone.

Man's Sin

After God created man and woman He gave them one command to follow. God charged them not to eat of the tree of the knowledge of good and evil. Adam and Eve had never known sin. The Bible teaches sin is lawlessness (1 Jn 3:4). They had never broken God's law so they were innocent and pure in the sight of God. Yet, they were tempted by Satan and ate from the forbidden tree, rebelling against their Creator and King. Their sin brought the judgement of God, and a curse on them both. The curse was death. Adam and Eve would now die physically and spiritually, that is, eternal death (commonly referred to as hell).

Jesus the Savior

The Bible says God loved the world so much He made a way for man to restore his broken relationship with his Creator. Because of sin, man is separated from God. God is perfect and can not have communion with an imperfect being. The only way man can be made right with God is to have his sins cleansed. Since man's sin makes him filthy in the sight of God, man can do nothing to cleanse himself. The only One who can cleanse man's sin is God Himself. To do this, God put on flesh through impregnating a Hebrew, virgin woman by His Spirit. Once born into the world, He lived a sinless life, died a sinner's death on a cross, and broke the curse of man's sin by rising from the grave after three days. God chose to humble Himself by taking on the form of His pinnacle creation (man) because of His abundant love.

Man's Response

God loves us and became a man to die for us, but to
receive forgiveness from your sins you *must* respond to Jesus' free gift of salvation. Jesus said a
man must be born again if he or she is to enter the
Kingdom of Heaven (Jn 3:3). To be born again you
must respond to God by placing your faith in Jesus
Christ. Faith is believing Jesus is the only true God,
and His life, death, and resurrection cleanse the
sins you have committed against His holy commands. You *must* also repent (turn-from your sins)
and pursue living obediently for your Creator and
Savior. If you genuinely believe in Christ for the forgiveness of your sins you will no longer be cast into
hell upon physical death, but you will now be saved
and welcomed into the Kingdom of God for all eternity. If you believe these words to be true, the Bible
says you can be sure of your salvation in *Romans*
10:9 through *"confess[ing] with thy mouth the Lord
Jesus, and... believe[ing] in thine heart that God hath
raised him from the dead, [and] thou shalt be saved."* I
encourage you to pray to God in faith. Ask Him to forgive you of your sins and truly begin to a lifestyle of
repentance. Also, I urge you to seek to know God
more by reading the Holy Bible daily.

The evangelistic Gospel presentation listed above *does not*
need to be repeated word for word, but the four points are a guide to
help you present the Gospel in a similar way as the apostles Paul and
Peter did in their lives on this side of the Kingdom (Ac 3; Rm 1-4).
The best way to present this format of the Gospel is to know your
Bible. When you know your Bible, you will be eager to use this format to share your faith. The evangelistic answer should be used
when you are trying to teach someone the Scriptures with the hopes
they will come to know God as their Creator and Savior. Though,
once someone does accept these truths, the full answer to this question should be the next step in helping them grow closer to the Lord
in their own life.

The Full Answer

The full answer to the question, What is the Gospel? is the whole Bible. **The whole Bible is the Gospel!** In *1 Corinthians* 15:3-4 Paul said, *"For I delivered unto you first of all that which I also received, how that Christ died for our sins according to the scriptures; And that he was buried, and that he rose again the third day according to the scriptures."* In these verses about the Gospel, Paul highlights the phrase *"according to the Scriptures"* twice. What is Paul saying here? He is telling us the rest of the Scriptures point to Christ. Likewise, after His resurrection, Jesus used all the Scriptures to teach His disciples about His death and resurrection (Lk 24:27). In the Bible God is telling a single story He wrote. The story begins with Creation in *Genesis* 1 and ends in the Kingdom of Heaven in *Revelation* 22.

If someone is really interested in knowing the full answer to the question, What is the Gospel? the best advice you can give them is to read and study the entire Bible again and again and again. Although many people have a Bible at home, they often find it too long or overwhelming to read. Others believe the Bible is not relevant to their lives, so they never open its pages to discover the riches of God's truth He has waiting to teach them. Still, others view the Bible as a fairytale.

My heart aches thinking about those who believe the Bible is irrelevant to their life for any reason. There is not a more relevant book in the world for every person on this planet. If you believe the Bible is irrelevant or if you have a dusty Bible at home or if you just do not understand how the Scriptures tie into your life then I am excited you are reading this book! *The Gospel Octagon* provides a biblical overview through teaching the entire story God began writing in *Genesis* 1 and is continuing to unfold in our daily lives. I hope *The Gospel Octagon* will be a useful aid to anyone seeking the truth of the Holy Bible.

Again, each and every Christian has been commanded by The Lord of all Creation to go and proclaim the Gospel (Mk 16:15). The short answer, the evangelistic answer, and the full answer are biblical blueprints helpful in presenting the Gospel to every creature.

Now, come with me as we unlock God's divine storyline by taking an in-depth look at the third answer - the *full* answer or what I call *The Gospel Octagon*...

INTRODUCTION

Throughout our world there are both literate and illiterate people professing Jesus Christ as God in every corner of the globe. From wealthy believers in New York City to impoverished believers in the slums of India, Christians bow to the one, true God. This aspect of Christianity is fascinating. **The truth of the Scriptures and man's relationship to our Creator pierce through the common divisions of men found in education, social status, and financial prosperity. God teaches *all* His children truth through the Scriptures and His Spirit, and the two always agree.** Every Christian, no matter their status in life, is responsible for the truths of God they hold in their hands. The Christian who has been taught more by God has more responsibility. So, the impoverished Christian living in the slums of India, owning a page of the Bible, if that, does not have the same level of responsibility as the wealthy Christian who possesses the entire Bible or five on their bookshelf (Dt 29:29; Mt 25:14-30; Lk 12:48). Interestingly, often the Christian with one page has more zeal to know God's Word than the Christian owning multiple versions in small, medium, and large print, or is leather bound with lavish illustrations. Those of us who have a Bible or access to one have an immense responsibility to know God's story and how we fit into His story. Moreover, Bible teachers have an even greater responsibility to teach the fullness of

God's story to their hearers, whether it be one person or one hundred million.

In my Christian life I have been taught God's Word by a variety of teachers. Although there are many healthy teaching ministries on the earth, my experience has taught me there are also many unhealthy ones. One way a teaching ministry can be unhealthy is through not teaching the Bible from *Genesis* to *Revelation*. This is very unbalanced and frustrating! Surprisingly, some ministries intentionally do not teach entire sections of the Bible. Those who do not teach the whole Bible leave their hearers confused, because they are leaving off main parts of the story. Think of it this way: When you tell a story, any story, there are different parts that make up the story's plot. In every story you have an introduction, rising action, climax, falling action, and to close the story, a resolution. Yet, the Bible's basic plot framework is not taught in many teaching ministries around the globe. Imagine watching only the climax of a movie, not the beginning, not the ending, just the climax...You would be utterly lost! The climax of a movie only makes sense as a part of the whole story. In the same way, you can not "watch" just the climax of God's story; It needs to be viewed in its *entirety* to be understood fully. Therefore, **the Gospel Octagon has been written to help teach an overview of God's *full story* in an easy, understandable way.**

Although there are many stories that make up the Bible's 66 books and letters, there is one continuous story throughout. If someone misses this truth they can easily misunderstand the Gospel. Misunderstanding the Gospel is detrimental to a healthy Christian life. My desire is to see Christians all over the world walk and grow to be healthy Christians. You might ask yourself, What is a healthy Christian? In my opinion, a healthy Christian is one who pursues living obediently for Jesus Christ in every area of their life.

My hope is that *The Gospel Octagon* will help you build a healthy theological framework for your Christian life.

The Bible is God's divine storyline and you have been written into His story! **Once we see ourself in God's narrative, our lives become caught up in the reality of who we are in Christ!** *The Gospel Octagon's* layout has eight sections, hence the octagon. The eight sections are:

1. Creation
2. Man's Sin
3. Israel
4. Jesus' 1st Coming
5. The Church
6. Jesus' 2nd Coming
7. Millennial Kingdom
8. Eternal Kingdom

These eight sections are the basic framework of the Bible. *The Gospel Octagon* begins with *Genesis* 1 and ends in *Revelation* 22. Each section is a major part of God's narrative. Every biblical story fits into one or more of these sections and thereby makes up the grand story God has written.

Here is a quick overview of the plot written by the very mind of God (Fig. .1). The Lord introduces His story by creating the heavens and the earth. Next, He takes a quick turn through rising action by telling of Man's Sin and His choosing to build the nation of Israel. Following that, God presents His first and main climax in the life, death, and resurrection of Jesus Christ to break the curse of sin. After Jesus' life on earth we see the birth of The Church and it represents the temporary falling action of the plot. God's second climax is Jesus' 2nd Coming to the earth to judge the wicked and honor the righteous. After this, the Millennial Kingdom resumes the falling action. Finally, God *ends* His glorious story by *beginning* the Eternal Kingdom. The combination of these eight sections and their distinctive details unveil God's divine storyline for the human age.

The Gospel Octagon Plot Line Graph

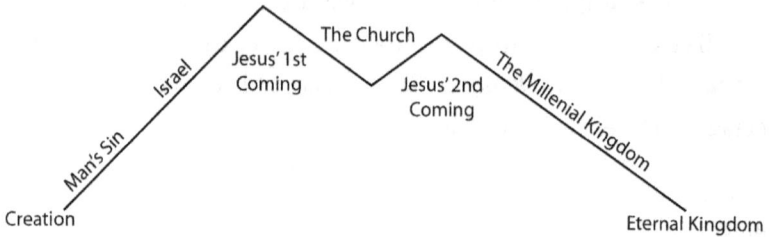

Fig. .1: A line graph displaying the eight sections of God's Divine Storyline.

Unfortunately, many churches today do not teach the whole Bible. Thus, many Christians, even regular church attendees, are unable to clearly see God's Gospel story line from beginning to end, which handicaps them in completely knowing and sharing the Gospel. Instead of teaching the whole Bible, many modern churches teach mostly on two of the eight sections: Jesus' 1st Coming and The Church.

Some might argue that teaching about Jesus' 1st Coming and The Church is the most important. Although their reasoning may be convincing at first thought, the truth comes to light when the full story is provided. Before we continue, let us remember *Proverbs* 18:17, which states, *"He that is first in his own cause seemeth just; but his neighbour cometh and searcheth him."* A biblical principle extracted from this proverb is: know the full story before determining a conclusion. Christians should be studious in analyzing people's words and not be led astray until having examined the whole story. Teaching one or two sections of the Bible does not teach the fullness of God's story. Christian leaders should be teaching the *whole* Bible. We must never believe someone's theology because they sound convincing without first understanding their perspective within the whole story God has written.

The entirety of the Bible needs to be taught regularly in order to develop healthy Christians. **Teaching ministries that focus mostly on one or two sections completely miss the importance of the fullness of the biblical story. Teaching about Jesus' 1st Coming and The Church are extremely important, but I want to stress that teaching these sections isolated from the other vital parts of Scripture *does not* help people learn the fullness of the Gospel story.**

The Holy Bible is the most stunning, glorious book that has ever been or ever will be written! The divine scriptures can be likened to a diamond cut to perfection. Just as a diamond has different facets which make up the fullness of its beauty, so also the fullness of the Bible's beauty is composed and revealed through every providential detail. *The Gospel Octagon* has the privilege of uncovering *some* of those details in God's breathtaking storyline. **The excitement begins at the very *beginning*, when The Eternal One spoke, bringing His story to life!**

Chapter One

CREATION

"In the beginning God created the heaven and the earth."

Genesis 1:1

The Story Line

God introduces His story by testifying of His Creation account. The introduction of the plot is all about God creating the heavens, the earth, and all He put on the earth. Undoubtedly, this section of God's story has been hijacked more than any other. The Creation section is the foundation of the rest of this book and it is truly the foundation of the Gospel of Jesus Christ.

The Beginning

Have you ever stopped to consider the wonder of your five senses? Each individual sense, in and of itself, is an incredible gift from God. **The combination of these senses produces the spectacular revelation that God created everything we see, touch, hear, smell, and taste, giving people the opportunity to experience The Lord's creation in a dynamic way!** Wow! God designed you with senses to enjoy His living art work! Let's think about this for a moment: Our eyes pierce the night sky peppered with distant lights that mesmerize children and adults alike. Our skin feels the warm affectionate embrace of another. Our ears hear the crunch of colorful maple leaves our feet trudge through in the autumn months. Our nose catches the aroma of hot, glazed cinnamon rolls just pulled out of the oven. Our tongue tastes the sweet flavor of sun-kissed blue berries, freshly picked. Yes, our five senses are themselves a testimony to God's stunning creation which surpasses human understanding. Creation is displayed for all to experience from the heavens to the earth, from the vastness of the universe to the complexity of a cell, from the skies above to the depths of the ocean, from plants to animals and from the seen to the unseen. Oh, and by the way, the Lord completed His art project in six days!

The Creator began His story by stating, *"In the beginning God created the heaven and the earth" (Gn 1:1).* This is one of the most simple, yet profound statements of all time. This first verse of the Bible is foundational to the Book of *Genesis*, and the whole Bible. **Having a healthy biblical worldview begins by understanding God created everything we experience with our five senses and *beyond!*** A worldview is how one sees and interprets the world, and their place in it. A *biblical* worldview begins with believing God created and therefore we and everything else exist. *Genesis*, the first book of the Bible, chapters one and two go on to describe the day-by-day account of the six-day creation. Knowing God created the heavens, the earth, and everything in them, including man, in six days is crucial for healthy Christian growth.

Six Day Creation

The first four words of the Bible are, *"In the beginning God"* *(Gn 1:1)*. These words signify God existed at the beginning of time. He created time! Knowing this to be true, we can conclude God existed before time and is therefore timeless (Is 40:28; Jn 17:24). In His goodness God created the heavens and the earth bringing about time, matter, and space as we understand them. The word *beginning* in *Genesis* 1:1 implies "God created the universe 'from nothing' (Latin *ex nihilo*)." Though this "text does not state" God created the universe from nothing, this truth is implied and confirmed in three passages of Scripture: *John* 1:3, *Romans* 4:17 and *Hebrews* 11:3.[4] For example, *John* 1:3 says, *"All things were made by him; and without him was not any thing made that was made."* "The emphasis in [*Genesis* 1:1] is on the origin of the universe. God created it. He alone is eternal, and everything else owes its origin and existence to Him."[5] After the first verse of the Bible, God continues to testify of His stunning creation using a day-by-day breakdown from earth's perspective... for the earth is the focus of all creation (Gn 1:1-2)!

Day 1

On the first day God created the heaven and the earth; the earth was formless because He had covered it in water. So when God created the earth it did not have visible land but was a water planet. Then He shined light onto planet earth and separated the light from the darkness calling the light *"day"* and the darkness *"night" (Gn 1:5)*. This marked the first day. At first you may think this light was the sun and the moon but it was not. The sun and moon were created on the fourth day. With that being the case, a good Bible student must ask, What was this light? There are different ideas about the light. One idea is this light refers to God shining His radiant, divine light into our universe. I like to think of this idea as though God is shining His light over the earth like a spotlight amongst the vastness of the universe saying, "This planet is special to me. Look at this story I am about to play out. The greatest story ever written will unfold on this water planet." Although we do not know for sure the specifics of what this light refers to, we do know it does not refer to the sun, moon, or stars because God specifically created those lights on the fourth day. Also, God used this light for the purpose of distinguishing between *day* and *night*. In other words, God is saying twenty-four hours have passed in the process of creating the heaven, the earth, and this unknown light that signified the day and night. We know the word *day* in *Genesis* 1 is a twenty-four hour day, because God tells us at the end of each day (for the first six days) there was an evening and a morning to mark each day. Furthermore, God reminds His people He created all things in six days later on in the story when He records the 10 commandments in *Exodus* 20:11. (To learn more from an expert on this subject I recommend reading Ken Ham's article, *Do The Days Really Matter?*, published in the Acts & Facts Magazine in 1990. You can find it on icr.org.)

Day 2

On the second day God created the sky by separating the earth waters which He created on day one. This separation is what we know today as the sky or the atmosphere. The earth was covered in water (a big sea) with the sky now separating a water filled atmosphere hovering above the waters below. (This topic will be discussed in further detail in Chapter Two.)

Day 3

On the third day God brought the waters (sea) together in one place so dry ground (land) would appear. This indicates the land could have been created on the first day and remained under the water but on this day the Lord made it appear. The other possibility is that God created the land on day three under the water. On this same day God created seed bearing trees and plant vegetation to burst forth from the ground to cover the face of the earth. At God's command, small grasses and giant tress and all kinds of luscious, edible vegetation began to rise from the dust of the earth, each producing fruits and seeds after their own kind.

Day 4

On the fourth day God created the sun, moon, and stars. You may ask yourself the logical question, If the sun, moon, and stars were created on the fourth day then how did the first three days have a evening and an morning (Gn 1:5; 8; 13)? Great question! The answer is these were twenty-four hour days without regard to the sun and moon. Remember God said, *"let there be light"* on day one (Gn 1:3). There was some sort of light, just not the lights (sun, moon, and stars) we are familiar with. I believe He created the sun, moon, and stars on the fourth day to show God is not subject to His creation, but rather His creation is subject to Him. You may also ask, How did the earth rotate without the gravitational pull from the sun that was not there for the first three days? God! He created everything and, yet, is subject to nothing! Another question you may ask is, How did the plants God created on day three grow without sunlight? The answer is simple, the plants grew because God caused them to grow by His Spirit. Again, **God is not limited by the physical laws He wrote!** The plants needed God for sustenance and He provided. Furthermore, I believe the plants grew very fast. They did not need a season to grow, like today. Rather, the plants simply needed God's Spirit. The One who created the seed does not need the natural process He set up for humans. He simply tells His creation what to do and it obeys.

Day 5

On the fifth day God created all the different kinds of slippery fish and sea life which swarm and scurry about in the waters. He then created all the kinds of aerodynamic birds which glide through the skies. *Genesis* 1:22 says, *"And God blessed them, saying, Be fruitful, and multiply, and fill the waters in the seas, and let fowl multiply in the earth."* In this verse God instructs all these animals He created to reproduce, filling the earth with an abundance of their own kind. Both fish and birds continue to fascinate people today! The abilities God gifted these animals with man does not possess, but even still our modern day technology tries to imitate their unmatched design and capabilities. Just about every person has thought about what it would be like to fly through the sky with ease like an eagle of the air, or to zoom through the waters at high speed like a dolphin of the sea. Both the creatures with fin and feather bring a mosaic of color and excitement into the earth. Animals of all kinds are special to God. **All His creatures bring Him glory by exposing His creative genius, for every one has been perfectly designed for a specific purpose.**

Day 6

On the sixth day God created the array of land animals, with each multiplying after the same kind. Then God did something uniquely different. He purposefully formed, from the dust of the earth, the first human being! After shaping this lifeless dust formation God did something even more wonderful. He breathed His own breath of life into it, bringing a man to life in His own image. Later that day God went on to create a woman for this man He named Adam. So we see here that **day six is a beautiful conclusion to God's masterpiece of creation in which Adam and Eve were given life upon the earth. These first two human beings were the only creations made in God's own image bearing God's breath of eternal life and having the freedom of choice with a soul.** God placed them in charge to reign over all of His creation. This man and woman were joined together in marriage in a perfect world. They walked with God, growing close to Him and one another in the paradise home He had placed them in, called the Garden of Eden. God loved, taught and blessed them. He told His children they were welcome to eat of the abundant produce in the garden, except for one particular tree. He stated the consequence of breaking the command was death (Gn 2:17). (We will expand more on this subject in the next chapter on Man's Sin.) After God's six-day creation was completed, "He called it all 'very good.' There was no death of *nephesh* creatures (*nephesh* is the Hebrew word referring to the life principle, or soul). People and animals were all vegetarian." [6]

There are many different interpretations of the six-day creation account. I believe God created the universe and our earth in six, twenty-four hour days. Some find this hard to believe, and rightly so since during the past couple hundred years evil men have been doing everything they can to distance themselves from God and His Word. After much brainwashing with the "millions and billions of years" that the earth and universe supposedly have existed, six, twenty-four hour days is a strange thought. But I believe God is faithful and His Word is reliable and is backed up by true science. But before we get there, let's take a closer look at how God's account of *His* creation is attacked in our world today.

Assault on Creation

Today, the truth of creation is under attack. This attack has come from those who propose the theory of evolution to be true. Sadly, evolution is being taught in schools across the world. Students of all ages are being brainwashed to believe this theory as fact. You may wonder what is so wrong with the theory of evolution. Simply put, this theory is a direct attack on the foundation of God's story. To clarify, evolution is the theory that in the beginning there was a big bang and over billions of years a single cell somehow developed. Then over many more unknown number of years this cell evolved into every living thing. In other words, this theory is an alternative view on how everything our five senses (and so much more!) experience came to be. The Bible says in the beginning God created all things. Evolutionists say in the beginning there was nothing and it exploded. Then, over a loooong period of time everything evolved to be what it is. Again, this idea is a direct attack on the biblical narrative of Creation. It is important to note, if evolutionists are correct, then the Bible would be false. Yet **the theory of evolution is not true, it is a lie. This lie is an embarrassment to the honest scientific community and anyone who values scientific facts.** Those who propose this theory to be fact support their theory with evidence which is not actually evidence that will hold up their theory! Let me explain how the lie is sold.

The lie begins with the mixing of two terms: *macro*evolution and *micro*evolution. Evolutionists teach macroevolution is true by supporting their theory with the evidence of microevolution. You may ask, What is macro and microevolution? Macroevolution is what is usually thought of when the word *evolution* is discussed. That is, in the beginning there was a big bang and everything we now see evolved from a single cell over billions of years into thousands of species. There is zero scientific evidence to support macroevolution. Since that is the case, evolutionists support their macroevolutionary theory by using the real scientific evidence found in microevolution. Microevolution, better known as adaptation, is the change of a species within its own kind. For example, dogs are bred to be small, tall, skinny, muscular, hairy, not so hairy, sweet, mean, and so forth. This is known as microevolution or adaptation. We see evidence of adaptation throughout the world. The key difference between macro and micro is that macroevolution has monkeys turning into man, whereas, microevolution only has monkeys becoming different kinds of monkeys based upon their genetics. Strangely enough, the evolutionists use microevolution to support the theory of macroevolution. This is absurd. Again, the reason microevolution is used to support macroevolution is because there is no evidence of macroevolution! Only, the evolutionists do not clarify the difference between macro and microevolution. They simply drop off the *macro* and *micro* and use the word *evolution*. Shame on all who are involved in this lie. Those who have spread this disastrous false teaching will be held responsible before God for misleading people away from trusting in His Word. More than anything, **the lie of macroevolution is sold with so much energy, passion, and money because it gives people a belief system which does not account for their sins, as the Creator of the heavens and earth does.** This belief system (religion) frees its followers from being held accountable to God. If people are not held accountable they can live a sinful lifestyle with no conviction, which is why moral relativism (the belief that morals are relative and not absolute) has grown exponentially in our society. Once people realize the theory of evolution is a farce, they can then begin to see clearly God created all we experience with our five senses (and so much more)!

"In the beginning God created" (Gn 1:1)! Knowing this truth lays the foundation for understanding God's story. He created all the wonders we encounter on a daily basis! Understanding God as the Creator is extremely important because without this first section there is no God. When there is no belief in the Creator God there are no absolute truths, so anything goes and nothing is wrong. On the other hand, when people believe in the Creator God they begin to have a desire within their spirit to know Him, the One and only true God and His Word. That is why teaching the fullness of the Bible, starting at the beginning, is so important. In our technological world many have rejected God, but there have been and still are many sci-

entists who follow Jesus Christ and use science to defend the truth of the Scriptures.

Creation Science

Science has confirmed the Bible is true time and time again. "The word *science* literally means 'knowledge'; it has its origin in the Latin term scire ('to know')."[7] Unfortunately, in our modern world, science has been used to manipulate and lie to people with regards to macroevolution and the age of the earth. In contrast to what some scientists believe, **the field of science is not a speculative philosophical subject that should be used to promote groundless theories.**[8] Rather, the field of science is the process of gaining knowledge from utilizing the scientific method. You may remember the basic, five-step research method you used growing up in your science classes to solve a problem.[9] The five steps are: observation, statement of the problem, proposal of a hypothesis, gathering of data through observation and experimentation, and formation of a conclusion. When the experiment has been completed, the scientist, will either prove their hypothesis to be true or false. If the hypothesis is repeatably proven true, then a scientific fact is proven. On the other hand, if the hypothesis is not proven, then the scientist forms a new hypothesis, starting the process over. The scientific method has been used by scientists, young and old, to learn more about the amazing and wonderful world God created.

Creation science is based on utilizing the scientific method with a biblical worldview. Those who do not start their scientific experiments with a biblical worldview start with another worldview, for there is no blank worldview. Since creation is an overwhelming testimony of The Creator, creation scientists believe true science begins with a biblical worldview, that is, believing the God of the Bible is true. Creation scientists, "can take comfort in the fact that many of the greatest scientists of the past were creationists"[10] who believed in the God of the Bible. "They believed that, as scientists, they were 'thinking God's thoughts after Him,' learning to understand and control the laws and processes of nature for God's glory and man's good."[11] They applied the scientific method in their search for understanding how God's creation works, just like *true* scientists today. "In fact one of them, Sir Francis Bacon, is credited with formulating and establishing the scientific method!"[12] Not only was he a creation scientist, but numerous fields of science got off the ground because Bible believing men sought to discover the truths of God's creation! Much of our modern age can be credited to men who were faithful to God, and believed the Bible to be true. God is the One who created the laws of mathematics, biology, physics, chemistry, and so on. **When man discovers something new, we are only learning more about God's creation.** That is what led, and still leads creation scientists to work hard in discovering more of God's stunning creation. Our modern world is indebted to creation scientists from the past, who not only made amazing discoveries, but opened entire fields of science (Fig. 1.1).[13]

SCIENTIFIC DISCIPLINES ESTABLISHED BY CREATIONIST SCIENTISTS

Discipline	Scientist
Antiseptic Surgery	Joseph Lister (1827-1912)
Bacteriology	Louis Pasteur (1822-1895)
Calculus	Isaac Newton (1642-1727)
Celestial Mechanics	Johann Kepler (1571-1630)
Chemistry	Robert Boyle (1627-1691)
Comparative Anatomy	Georges Cuvier (1769-1832)
Computer Science	Charles Babbage (1792-1871)
Dimensional Analysis	Lord Rayleigh (1842-1919)
Dynamics	Isaac Newton (1642-1727)
Electronics	John Ambrose Fleming (1849-1945)
Electrodynamics	James Clerk Maxwell (1831-1879)
Electro-Magnetics	Michael Faraday (1791-1867)
Energetics	Lord Kelvin (1824-1907)

Entomology of Living Insects	Henri Fabre (1823-1915)
Field Theory	Michael Faraday (1791-1867)
Fluid Mechanics	George Stokes (1819-1903)
Galactic Astronomy	William Herschel (1738-1822)
Gas Dynamics	Robert Boyle (1627-1691)
Genetics	George Mendel (1822-1884)
Glacial Geology	Louis Agassiz (1807-1873)
Gynecology	James Simpson (1811-1870)
Hydraulics	Leonardo Da Vinci (1452-1519)
Hydrography	Matthew Maury (1806-1873)
Hydrostatics	Blaise Pascal (1623-1662)
Ichthyology	Louis Agassiz (1807-1873)
Isotopic Chemistry	William Ramsay (1852-1916)
Model Analysis	Lord Rayleigh (1842-1919)
Natural History	John Ray (1627-1705)
Non-Euclidean Geometry	Bernhard Riemann (1826-1866)
Oceanography	Matthew Maury (1806-1873)
Optical Mineralogy	David Brewster (1781-1868)
Paleontology	John Woodward (1665-1728)
Pathology	Rudolph Virchow (1821-1902)
Physical Astronomy	Johann Kepler (1571-1630)
Reversible Thermodynamics	James Joule (1818-1889)
Statistical Thermodynamics	James Clerk Maxwell (1831-1879)
Stratigraphy	Nicholas Steno (1631-1686)
Systematic Biology	Carolus Linnaeus (1707-1778)
Thermodynamics	Lord Kelvin (1824-1907)
Thermokinetics	Humphrey Davy (1778-1829)
Vertebrate Paleontology	Georges Cuvier (1769-1832)

Fig. 1.1: A two-column table showing scientific disciplines that were started by creation scientists and the date of their birth and death. This table was put together by the Institute for Creation Research ministry. Their website is icr.org.[14]

This list of creation scientists is impressive! Their achievements paved the way for our modern technological world. Sadly, creation scientists are a minority in today's scientific community. Their voices are silenced and even scoffed at by many scientists, which is ironic given that today's modern science arose from a biblical foundation.[15] Still, there are numerous scientists today, like the men listed, who believe the Bible to be fully true and scientifically accurate. The *Institute for Creation Research* is a wonderful scientifically based ministry that focuses on proclaiming the truth of God's creation through science. You can learn more about their work at icr.org. Another great ministry in this field of study is *Creation Today*. You can learn more about their work at creationtoday.org.

Dinosaurs

Dinosaurs are extraordinary! God created so many amazing creatures, but there is something unique about dinosaurs and they play an important role in the truth of God's Word found in the first chapter of *Genesis*. All land animals were created on the sixth day, including dinosaurs! Some of these dinosaurs were massive! I believe God refers to them in *Genesis* 1:24, when He said He created the *"beast[s] of the earth."* Truly, dinosaurs are a wonder and powerfully testify of God's creativeness in the animal kingdom.

Dinosaurs In The Bible

Did you know the word *dinosaur,* which means "terrifying lizard," was invented in 1841?[16] Prior to this date dinosaurs were often referred to as dragons or serpents by people all around the world. In fact, the word *dragon* is used 35 times in 34 verses in 10 different books of the *King James Bible*, which was published in the year 1611. That is 230 years before the word *dinosaur* was invented! This has importance because the translators who wrote the first English version of the Bible (1611 KJV) used the word *dragon* to describe what we term today as dinosaur, since the word *dinosaur* had not yet been invented![17] Dinosaurs and dragons are one in the same and are in the Bible!

There are three different meanings for the word *dragon* in the Bible. First, the word *dragon* is used in poetry to suggest something related to dragons. For example, in *Job* 30:29 Job said *"I am a brother to dragons, And a companion to owls."* In context, Job meant that in his present nightmarish condition, he felt more akin to dragons and owls than he did to other people. He had lost sight of close friends who loved him and built him up, and so he expressed himself by saying he felt like a wild animal. Too, maybe he said this because dragons are scary and everyone runs from them, and that is how he felt due to his physical appearance.

Second, the word *dragon* is used to reference Satan, especially in the book of *Revelation*. For example, *Revelation* 12:3; 9 says *"And there appeared another wonder in heaven; and behold a great red dragon, having seven heads and ten horns, and seven crowns upon his heads." "And the great dragon was cast out, that old serpent, called the Devil, and Satan, which deceiveth the whole world: he was cast out into the earth, and his angels were cast out with him."* Clearly, the dragon here is referring to Satan.

Lastly, the word *dragon* is used in a very literal sense to describe dinosaurs. I believe *at least* nine of the 35 times the word *dragon* is used in the Bible it is referencing real dinosaurs. These verses noticeably speak about dinosaurs archeologists have actually dug up in our modern times. You know, those ginormous bones which cause eyes to pop and jaws to drop in young and old in museums throughout the world. Let's take a closer look at six of these verses.

> *"Thou shalt tread upon the lion and adder: the young lion and the **dragon** shalt thou trample under feet."*
>
> *Psalm 91:13*

> *"And the wild beasts of the islands shall cry in their desolate houses, and **dragons** in their pleasant palaces: and her time is near to come, and her days shall not be prolonged."*

Isaiah 13:22

And thorns shall come up in her palaces, nettles and brambles in the fortresses thereof: and it shall be an habitation of dragons, and a court for owls.

Isaiah 34:13

The beast of the field shall honour me, the dragons and the owls: because I give waters in the wilderness, and rivers in the desert, to give drink to my people, my chosen. This people have I formed for myself; they shall shew [show] forth my praise.

Isaiah 43:20-21

And the wild asses [donkeys] did stand in the high places, they snuffed up the wind like dragons; their eyes did fail, because there was no grass.

Jeremiah 14:6

Therefore I will wail and howl, I will go stripped and naked: I will make a wailing like the dragons, and mourning as the owls.

Micah 1:8

Sadly, western culture teaches dragons are mythical creatures. As you read through those six verses, What came to your mind? Does the Bible seem to be describing a mythical creature or a real animal God created? In these verses the dragon(s) is/are referred to alongside other animals modern people are familiar with. Did you catch them? There are four animals mentioned by name and a group of animals called wild beasts. The four mentioned by name are: lion, adder (small snake), owls, and asses (donkeys). So you can see that while God spoke about dinosaurs (dragons) in the Bible, He does so alongside other animals we are familiar with even today. In doing so, God seems to be affirming the dragon is just as real a creature as the others. Does it make more sense to describe these dragons as mythical or real? The answer is clear that God in-

tended us to understand dragons (dinosaurs) as real creatures. God
provides even further evidence in Scripture we can glean from. Let's
continue to look deeper!

There are a couple examples where God specifically names
different kinds of dragons and describes them in great detail. In *Job*
40 God spends nine verses describing the mightiest land creature
He created during the creation week: the Sauropod dinosaur! Here
is the record of God's Word to Job,

> *Moreover the Lord answered Job, and said, Shall he that*
> *contendeth with the Almighty instruct him? he that re-*
> *proveth God, let him answer it. Then Job answered the*
> *Lord, and said, Behold, I am vile; what shall I answer*
> *thee? I will lay mine hand upon my mouth. Once have I*
> *spoken; but I will not answer: yea, twice; but I will pro-*
> *ceed no further. Then answered the Lord unto Job out of*
> *the whirlwind, and said, Gird up thy loins now like a*
> *man: I will demand of thee, and declare thou unto*
> *me. Wilt thou also disannul my judgment? wilt thou con-*
> *demn me, that thou mayest be righteous? Hast thou an*
> *arm like God? or canst thou thunder with a voice like*
> *him? Deck thyself now with majesty and excellency; and*
> *array thyself with glory and beauty. Cast abroad the rage*
> *of thy wrath: and behold every one that is proud, and*
> *abase him. Look on every one that is proud, and bring*
> *him low; and tread down the wicked in their place. Hide*
> *them in the dust together; and bind their faces in*
> *secret. Then will I also confess unto thee that thine own*
> *right hand can save thee.* **Behold now behemoth, which**
> **I made with thee; he eateth grass as an ox. Lo now, his**
> **strength is in his loins, and his force is in the navel of**
> **his belly. He moveth his tail like a cedar: the sinews of**
> **his stones are wrapped together. His bones are as**
> **strong pieces of brass; his bones are like bars of**
> **iron. He is the chief of the ways of God: he that made**
> **him can make his sword to approach unto him. Surely**
> **the mountains bring him forth food, where all the**
> **beasts of the field play. He lieth under the shady trees,**
> **in the covert of the reed, and fens. The shady trees**
> **cover him with their shadow; the willows of the brook**
> **compass him about. Behold, he drinketh up a river, and**

hasteth not: he trusteth that he can draw up Jordan into his mouth. He taketh it with his eyes: his nose pierceth through snares.

Job 40:1-24

In the fifteenth verse of this passage The Lord began to describe this giant creature by instructing Job, *"Look now at the behemoth."* Due to the lie of evolution, many people have doubted that the biblical behemoth is indeed a dinosaur. Some Bible commentaries embarrassingly suggest this animal to be a hippopotamus, an elephant, an alligator, or is just mythical altogether. As we look closer at the text you will see why these conclusions are not compatible with the truth of God's description. Before we start, note God describes 10 other kinds of animals to Job right before the passage expounding upon the great behemoth. This giant is listed right alongside all the other non-mythical creatures. Why would God include a "mythical animal" in with other animals that are still alive today? Was He being deceptive or speaking plainly about animals He created with man on day six? **We know God is never deceptive, that is Satan's job who uses men to twist God's Word.** God was speaking plainly! **Dinosaurs were created with and lived alongside of man!**

Now, we will examine the physical characteristics of the behemoth described in *Job 40:15-18.* This will help us determine what kind of animal this was, and eliminate what it was not. There are eight pieces of evidence confirming, without question, God is describing the largest land animal He ever created. The eight evidences are:

1. God informs us the behemoth eats grass. This highlights the animal is most likely vegetarian.

2. The behemoth has strength in his hips.

3. The behemoth has power in his stomach muscles.

4. The behemoth moves his tail like a cedar.

5. The behemoth's bones are like beams of bronze.

6. The behemoth has ribs like bars of iron.

7. In the nineteenth verse of this passage God informs the reader that this creature *"is the chief of the ways of God."* The Hebrew word for *chief* is *reshith* and it can mean beginning, chief, choice, choicest, finest, first, finest, foremost. It seems as though God was saying,[18] "This is the chief or the greatest (in size) land animal I created. There is no other that compares."

8. God goes on to say in verse twenty-three that this behemoth was such an incredibly powerful creature it could even stand in a raging river and not be moved.

The only creature known to man that accounts for all eight of these descriptions is the grandest dinosaur of them all: The giant Sauropod dinosaur! In 2006 the largest skeleton of a Sauropod was unearthed. The archeologist, Kenneth Lacovara, named the dinosaur Dreadnoughtus schrani. It's sheer size in weight is bigger than a massive Boeing 737-900 airplane by over 20 tons![19] (Check out the visual aid in Fig. 1.2 to put this stunning fact into perspective![20])

The Behemoth Dinosaur

Size & Weight Comparisions for *Dreadnoughtus schrani*

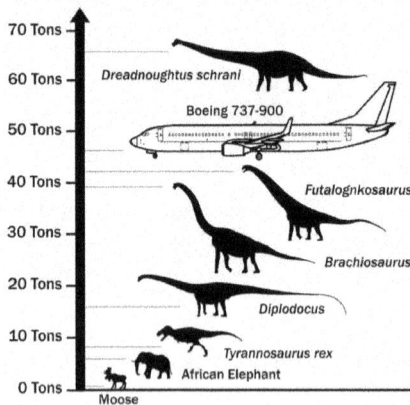

References and image attributions here:
https://www.dropbox.com/s/l4agkq0q91ylcmq/Dreadnoughtus%20Size%20Chart%20Attributions.docx?dl=0

Fig. 1.2: The Dreadnoughtus schrani is the largest dinosaur ever discovered. The length of this dinosaur measures 85 feet long and it would have weighed about 65 tons.[21]

Dinosaurs & Human Artifacts

Our current world lives and breathes by the latest information. We have come to love what is new, exciting, marketable, and ultimately sellable. That's right, people love what sells and nothing is sold without an agenda. Sometimes the agenda is to make money. Sometimes the agenda is political. Sometimes the agenda is faith based. And sometimes the agenda is a combination of all of these categories and more.

In schoolrooms, books, t.v. shows, and movies we are taught (input the word *sold* for taught or *brainwashed* might be a better fit) that dinosaurs lived well over 25 million years ago. Remember, there is an agenda for why the public is being sold this line and a lot of people are in on the lie. Sadly, many who push this agenda really believe this lie because it's what they were taught. Most people don't take the time to think, but would rather believe by faith their teachers' or college professors' word. We hope this book will help you think and evaluate the evidence rather than believe a lie. Different people have their own agendas, but in the end **the "millions of years" agenda is satanic because it causes many to reject God.** If dinosaurs really did live 25-200 million years ago, we must ask ourself the following question: Why are there cave paintings, pottery, sculptures, wall carvings, and other records of man's knowledge of dinosaurs throughout the earth?[22] Not only are we falsely told dinosaurs lived millions of years ago, we are also wrongly taught man came into existence no more than 100,000 years ago. According to the mainstream account of history, man and dinosaurs lived millions of years apart, which means man never lived with dinosaurs! Clearly, we have a HUGE problem on our hands with the data presented to us, and the observational scientific facts we know today.

Are you familiar with the artifacts discovered bearing proof of man and dinosaur living together? This might be the first time you have ever heard such a claim. There is abundant evidence man and dinosaurs walked together, disproving the popular "science" claims that dinosaurs existed millions of years ago. Here are a three well known artifacts to prove this scientific fact (Fig. 1.3 - 1.5).

Stegosaurus Dinosaur Carving

Fig. 1.3: A dinosaur carving of a "stegosaur-like creature" found on an 800 year old temple in Cambodia. This picture was taken by Don Patton.[23]

Sauropod Dinosaur Pottery

Fig. 1.4: This is "the Narmer Palette, which dates back to about 3,100 BC. It is from the ancient Egyptian capital of Hierakonpolis and shows the triumph of King Narmer with long necked dragons that appear to be in captivity."[24]

Ica Stone

Fig. 1.5: This is "an Ica Ceremonial Burial Stone from the Nasca culture" dating back to "100 BC to 800AD." The anatomical accuracy of this carving (straight legs and raised tail) has stood firm through the attacks of evolutionists. In the 1960s Paleontologists believed "dinosaurs dragged their tales." Today, they believe they did not and are in agreement with the Icas![25]

How could ancient people know the anatomy of a living dinosaur which had become extinct millions of years before they came into existence? They could not! If dinosaurs lived prior to man's existence, as modern science teaches, **Why is there observational scientific evidence all over the earth confirming dinosaurs and man lived at the same time?** The answers to these questions are obvious, unless of course, one is choosing to be deceived. The people making these artifacts had a thorough knowledge of dinosaurs and their anatomical structures. **Man did live alongside dinosaurs! God created them both on the sixth day thousands of years ago, not millions!**

Dinosaur Soft Tissue Discovered

In January of 2004, a paleontologist, Mary Schweitzer, was the first to discover soft tissue inside a Tyrannosaurus Rex thighbone supposed to be 65 million years old![26] Since her discovery, many similar ones have been made.[27] Again, we have to ask ourselves, How is this possible since living tissues can not last for that ridiculous length of time?[28] The answer is simple. Man and dinosaurs lived together at the same time. Fig. 1.6 is a picture of the Tyrannosaurus' soft tissue!

Tyrannosaurus Rex Soft Tissue

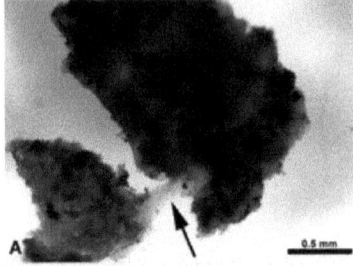

Fig. 1.6: Microscopic picture of Mary Schwitzer's Tyrannosaurs Rex "soft, pliable tissue [discovered] inside the bone!"[29]

In recapping, the scientific evidence about dinosaurs declares the Bible is clearly describing *actual* dinosaurs, archeological evidence of man and dinosaurs living together, and current discoveries confirm dinosaurs lived thousands, not millions, of years ago!

The Grand Engineer

Engineering is a branch of science which focuses on design and construction, ranging from tremendously big projects like skyscrapers to remarkably small projects like invisible computers. Designing a large building or a nano-computer takes a lot of planing and hard work. Whether people look at a painting, a building, or a computer they instinctively know there was an intelligent mind at work in designing and producing the painting, the building, and the computer. Design testifies of a designer. Likewise, **creation cries out there is a Creator**, since everything within creation is clearly designed! Creation testifies of the engineering marvel of our great King, Jesus! God is the Grand Engineer! From the immensely large size of the universe to extremely small size of a cell, God's design is unimaginably complex. To help us peak into God's creation, let's examine four different parts, starting with the HUGE and then proceeding to the tiny.

The Universe

According to modern scientists, there are between 100 to 200 billion galaxies in the universe.[30] That is a lot! Did you notice they use 100 billion as the skewed range? Wow, that is a huge range! Even though man prides himself on knowledge, when astrophysicist's skew is 100 billion, it shows how little they really know. Either way, God created a lot of galaxies that are beyond man's comprehension and they show us how small we are in the midst of His creation.

The galaxy earth resides in is called the Milky Way Galaxy. Amazingly, our sun is one of 100 to 400 billion stars within the Milky Way.[31] The sun, the star our solar system revolves around, is so large over one million earth's could fit inside it![32]

The Earth

Planet earth is the most special planet in the vastness of the universe. Our home is "the only planet known to contain living organisms." On average, our planet is 93 million miles from the sun. The surface of earth is roughly 70% water. The atmosphere of the earth, created on day two, protects living tissue from being damaged through the suns' radiation. As well, earth's magnetic field helps to protect life from damaging radiation. According to Dr. Jason Lisle, the Director of Physical Sciences at the Institute for Creation Research (ICR),

> The strength of the magnetic field has been slowly but continually dropping since scientists have been able to measure it nearly two centuries ago. This drop is consistent with earth's biblical age of around

6,000 years but is wildly inconsistent with the secular assumption of billions of years.

As well, the axis of the earth is tilted at 23.4 degrees in relation to its yearly solar orbit, which is why the earth has four seasons. Dr. Lisle continues by adding,

> This tilt appears to be well-designed for life. If earth were tilted less, the polar regions would receive less energy, reducing the habitable area of the planet. If the earth were tilted more, the seasons would become more extreme, potentially reducing the plant-growing season and making the environment less hospitable.

Of all the planets in the universe, God specially designed the earth for life. "God chose to spend five of the six days of creation working on earth, making it just the way He wanted it to be. All the other planets were created in one day: day four."[33]

The Human Body

On the sixth day, God created Adam and Eve, the pinnacle of His creation, in the very image of Himself! The human body is fascinating! Each body has billions of working parts that work together every day. There are 206 bones and 639 muscles which "enable it to move with incredible split-second timing"[34] Whether it be a petite young lady drifting through the air as she dances ballet with ease, or an oversized muscular body builder bursting out of his clothes as he lifts hundreds of pounds, the human body has been designed to master a variety of movements. Here are some more interesting facts about the amazing human body!

Dr. Jerry Bergman, a contributor to ICR's *Acts & Facts* magazine and former atheist,[35] has the following to say about the body that only God could have designed: "For eating and in-between, in every twenty-four hour period, the average person swallows about 2,000 times. Our heart beats over 100,000 times daily to move blood 168 million miles around our body." The doctor goes on to write, "We take about 23,800 breaths per day to bring 438 cubic feet of air to our lungs." Regarding our sense of hearing he records, "The human ear with its 24,000 'hair cells' which convert vibrations to electrical impulses, is capable of hearing sounds of astonishing low level acoustic energy."[36] Regarding the fuel needed to run our bodies the doctor notes,

> To work this marvelous machine, we need energy and building materials. Our three and one half pounds of daily food intake is chewed by 32 teeth (one of our most precious possessions) where it is mixed by saliva, a mild digestant secreted from five glands located in the mouth area.

Dr. Bergman highlights the complexity of God's design within the human body by adding,

> The body has a chemical plant far more intricate than any plant that man has ever built. This plant changes the food we eat into living tissue. It causes the growth of flesh, blood, bones and teeth. It even repairs the body when parts are damaged by accident or disease.[37]

The doctor understands that "The whole body system functions as a unified whole to enable a human to run, sing, remember, create and achieve the myriads of other phenomenal tasks we usually take for granted."[38] "Yes, the human body is a wonderful machine. The fact that any one of these devices exists is a complete demonstration that they are the work of an intelligent and [skillful] designer, God Himself."[39]

The Cell

Cells are what run everything! During God's creation week, He formed the plants, animals, and two people through giving each of them individualized coded directions in their complex cells. Research has shown the human body contains around 100 trillion cells.[40] We have about 200 different types of cells in our body.[41] From our muscles to our liver to our teeth to our skin, our cells are tiny living programs. One cell is programmed to create skin. Another cell is programmed to create tears to keep your eyelids gliding smoothly. Other cells grow hair to protect your first layer of armor, your skin cells. Still, other cells create feeling all over your body and some cells are even programmed to bring you pleasure. A single cell operates like an extremely complex manufacturing factory. Each part of the cell has been programed by God to operate in a specific way. Cells contain DNA, the genetic information necessary for directing cellular activities. DNA, the basic building block of life, is a long molecule containing four chemical bases: adenine (A), guanine (G), thymine (T), and cytosine (C).[42] Each cell contains six billion steps of DNA.[43] An individual piece of "DNA can be stretched six feet, but it is coiled up in the cell's nucleus, which measures only 1/2500 of an inch in diameter."[44]

God is the Great Engineer! In just six days He created countless breathtaking wonders we observe every day. We've lightly scratched the surface of only four! I encourage you to study out more, think often on the wonders of creation, and glorify our Creator for His stunning designs!

Creation is the biblical introduction of God's divine story line. The foundation for understanding the rest of God's story was laid down in the first two chapters of *Genesis*. It is a firm and spectacular beginning to the greatest story ever written by the heart of God. Now let us continue onward following the rising action of this plot as it takes unexpected, phenomenal, and world changing turns through the next two sections, Man's Sin and Israel.

Chapter Two

MAN'S SIN

"...she [Eve] took of the fruit thereof, and did eat, and gave also unto her husband with her; and he did eat. And the eyes of them both were opened, and they knew that they were naked; and they sewed fig leaves together, and made themselves aprons."

Genesis 3:6,7

The Story Line

After God introduces His story by testifying of His Creation account, the rising action of the plot follows, including both this chapter and the next about Israel. From here, the plot intensifies. This section focuses on the origin of sin and its escalation throughout God's story.

Original Sin

On the sixth day of the creation week, God finished His work with a crescendo by forming Adam and Eve! Upon completing His work, God proclaimed everything very good (Gn 1:31)! Adam and Eve were unique among all of God's creation; They were the only ones made in the image of God. For this reason God gave them and their descendants dominion over all He had made. They were blessed to learn from God Himself in the Garden of Eden. He was their King. The One who loved them, taught them, and blessed them abundantly. God had created a paradise: A heaven on earth! But everything was about to change...

Adam and Eve were pure and without sin at creation. When God placed them in their paradise, He gave them but one law to follow. **The Bible tells us sin is breaking God's laws (1 Jn 3:4).** Now that there was "a law in the books," the opportunity to break it had begun. The one and only command and its consequence God gave to Adam and Eve is found in *Genesis* 2:16-17 which reads,

> *And the Lord God commanded the man, saying, Of every tree of the garden thou mayest freely eat: But of the tree of the knowledge of good and evil, thou shalt not eat of it: for in the day that thou eatest thereof thou shalt surely die.*

Adam and Eve walked in communion with God in the Garden of Eden and knew His law and also the consequence of breaking His law. They lived in paradise. There was no sickness, pain, hurt, lies, heartache, adultery, betrayal, selfishness, theft, blasphemy, murder, or even death. They had lush fruits and vegetables to eat and their bodies were strong, fit, and healthy! They enjoyed life, loving and growing in their relationship with God and one another!

Although the first two people had everything they could ever need at their disposal, the third chapter of *Genesis* reveals a sharp turn in God's story which changed the course of history forever. The sharp twist includes Satan. Throughout the scriptures we learn Satan is a fallen angel, i.e. an angel in the Kingdom of Heaven that was kicked out because of his rebellion (sin) against God. Although Satan was kicked out, the Lord has used this wicked being for His own purpose in the lives of men.

Before we explore the specifics of Adam and Eve's sin, let's answer two questions many people today ask. One, Why did God put the tree in the Garden of Eden? Two, Why did God allow Satan to temp His creation? The answer to both of these questions is much the same. God put the tree in the garden and allowed Satan to temp His creation because God is after people who will love Him freely. If there was no tree, then there would be no law to break. Since there would be no law to break, the question arises, How could we know and prove we genuinely love God? **If people do not have an opportunity to reject God, then they do not have the opportunity to love Him. People can only love when there is an opportunity to not love. Love is a choice.** Again, if there was no law to break, then there would be no opportunity to choose to obey. If there was no choice to obey, then there would be no love. Without love God would only have robots He programmed to obey Him. Love can not be forced; love must be chosen. God chose to provide us with the opportunity to choose Him or reject Him. He desires people who will genuinely love Him when they have the opportunity to not love.

The tree in the garden and Satan are vital parts of the story God has written. His purpose was to create a world where Adam and Eve and you and I would have the opportunity to choose to obey Him or reject Him. We get to make the choice. **When people**

choose to freely love God when there is the opportunity to reject Him, genuine love is made.

In *Genesis* 3 Satan enters the story as a serpent and begins speaking his deception by entering into dialogue with Eve.

Now the serpent was more subtil than any beast of the field which the Lord God had made. And he said unto the woman, Yea, hath God said, Ye shall not eat of every tree of the garden?

And the woman said unto the serpent, We may eat of the fruit of the trees of the garden: But of the fruit of the tree which is in the midst of the garden, God hath said, Ye shall not eat of it, neither shall ye touch it, lest ye die.

And the serpent said unto the woman, Ye shall not surely die: For God doth know that in the day ye eat thereof, then your eyes shall be opened, and ye shall be as gods, knowing good and evil.

And when the woman saw that the tree was good for food, and that it was pleasant to the eyes, and a tree to be desired to make one wise, she took of the fruit thereof, and did eat, and gave also unto her husband with her; and he did eat.

Genesis 3:1-6

This passage of Scripture is vital in understanding Satan's primary means of deception. He still uses the same tactic today that he did in the beginning: He attacks the very Words of God (Gn 3:4). God told Adam and Eve death would be the consequence of breaking His law. Eve had this knowledge. She even affirmed God's Word to Satan, yet, he declared to Eve God was a liar, and Eve would surely not die if she disobeyed God. Sadly, as the passage above reveals, both Adam and Eve followed Satan's advice, committing high treason against their Creator and King. Their decision brought an abrupt change in God's script which altered the course of life on earth for thousands of years.

Immediately after their rebellion, Adam and Eve experienced a dramatic shift from the life they once knew by feeling shame at their nakedness. Prior to that time, they had no acquaintance with feelings of shame, guilt, and fear. These were new and revolting experiences. They felt shame because they broke God's law. Also, they had knowledge of good and evil, and now knew of their sin and were frightened at the extent of the repercussions to come. Their gripping fear caused them to hide from God, their Friend, the One whom they had walked with in perfect union. God had informed them the consequence of violating His command was death.

Once they ate the forbidden fruit, Adam and Eve knew clearly they and their descendants would physically die on the earth (Gn 3:19). Not only did their sin cause them to one day die physically, but their sin also caused spiritual death (Gn 2:17; 2 Th 1:7-9). Spiritual death began with a breaking of their fellowship with God in the Garden of Eden, but it did not end there. Spiritual death continued upon their earthly physical death. Once they physically died, their eternal spirit would be separated from the Creator of life forever. In essence, God would turn His back on them because they were stained with sin, something God can not abide to have in His presence, for He is holy. The Bible doesn't clearly reveal the extent of Adam and Eve's knowledge of their *eternal* spiritual death, yet, they did have clear knowledge of their *earthly* spiritual death on earth. We see this in Scripture because their communion with God was broken when they were kicked out of the Garden of Eden away from God's presence, and He cursed them (Gn 3).

The Gospel Octagon holds the position that Adam and Eve had *full* knowledge of their eternal spiritual death apart from God intervening in some way. The main reason I believe this is because their children begin making sacrifices to the Lord. Cain and Abel's sacrifices reveal their knowledge of appeasing God's wrath, something God later records in the Scriptures (Gn 4:1-5; Lv 4:35; 5:10). The only way Adam and Eve's descendants could have known to do this would be because God revealed this to them.

Cain & Abel

The first natural born son of the earth was Cain, named by his parents, Adam and Eve. His younger brother was named Abel. When they grew up, Cain became a farmer and Abel a shepherd. Both brothers grew up under their parents leadership learning about God, the Garden of Eden, sin and the consequences sin brought into the world. As grown men, both Cain and Abel presented sacrifices to the Lord for their sins as they had been instructed by their parents. *Genesis* 4:3-7 reads,

> *And in process of time it came to pass, that Cain brought of the fruit of the ground an offering unto the Lord. And Abel, he also brought of the firstlings of his flock and of the fat thereof. And the Lord had respect unto Abel and to his offering: But unto Cain and to his offering he had not respect. And Cain was very wroth, and his countenance fell. And the Lord said unto Cain, Why art thou wroth? and why is thy countenance fallen? If thou doest well, shalt thou not be accepted? and if thou doest not well, sin lieth at the door. And unto thee shall be his desire, and thou shalt rule over him.*

Both of these men presented a sacrifice to the Lord, which is an act of worship. Verse three says, *"...Cain brought of the fruit of the ground an offering"*, but *"...Abel, he also brought of the firstlings of his flock and of the fat thereof."* What is different in these offerings? Well, "Cain brought the work of his hands as a sacrifice to God. His actions became a prototype of false religion throughout the ages. The essential elements have always been the same: refusing God's sacrificial plan, attempting to atone for their mistakes through a system of good works."[45] On the other hand, "Abel offered a blood sacrifice and demonstrated his obedience to God's plan. He earned God's respect, not because his right actions atoned for his sin, but because the principle of substitutionary sacrifice was employed."[46] A blood sacrifice is necessary to cover sins, and they knew this. Therefore, God rejected Cain but accepted Abel. God's rejection of Cain's offering caused Cain to become sad. Afterward, the Lord told Cain he would be accepted if he did what was right. God warned Cain about sin and its eagerness to control him, and The Lord encouraged Cain to reject sin in his life.

In the next few verses of chapter four, Cain makes his decision, following in the footsteps of his parents rebellion.

> *And Cain talked with Abel his brother: and it came to pass, when they were in the field, that Cain rose up against Abel his brother, and slew him. And the Lord said unto Cain, Where is Abel thy brother? And he said, I know not: Am I my brother's keeper? And he said, What hast thou done? the voice of thy brother's blood crieth unto me from the ground. And now art thou cursed from the earth, which hath opened her mouth to receive thy brother's blood from thy hand;*

> *Genesis 4:8-12*

Clearly, Cain did not heed God and reject the temptation to sin. Rather, out of jealousy, Cain abandoned God's Word and chose to murder his brother, Abel. Although we are unable to read the words Satan whispered into Cain's ear, one wonders what role He played in this horrible affair.

The first child to be born on earth was a murderer. Instead of shedding the blood of a lamb for his sins, Cain chose to shed the blood of his brother in sin. Cain's actions displayed his anger-filled, disobedient heart. This story shows us the quick escalation of sinful man after the rebellion of Adam and Eve in the Garden of Eden. From this point forward, the sinful nature of humanity continues to grow as Satan deceives man from living for God.

Noah

One interesting component found in the Bible is the genealogical record, in which Noah, son of Lemech, is found to be the
ninth descendent from Adam. These records not only record genealogical names, but also the age each of our forefathers lived to, beginning with Adam and ending with Judah, son of Jacob. These are
valuable records revealing fascinating treasures of knowledge, yet so
often they get overlooked! One such treasure is **Adam, the first
man God created, lived for 930 years!** Wow! That's a long
time! Another treasure found is Noah's dad, Lemech, was born when
Adam was 874 years old. Simple arithmetic reveals Adam was alive
for the first 56 years of Lemech's life. Could you imagine all Adam
could have taught Lemech during those 56 years? Remember, Adam
walked with God in the Garden of Eden. He was probably the smart-
est man ever to have lived on earth. Given his age, he was able to
pass his wisdom to each generation, even into Lemech's life. As the
Genesis record shows, during the first two thousand years of history
people lived a long, long time compared to lifespans today.

In *Genesis* 6 we find the record of Noah and how God used
this man in our history. Noah had listened to the godly advice he
had heard passed down from his ancestor, Adam. Sadly, when Noah
was around 500 years old, *"God saw that the wickedness of man was
great in the earth, and that every imagination of the thoughts of his heart
was only evil continually" (Gn 6:5). "The earth also was corrupt before
God, and the earth was filled with violence" (Gn 6:11).* The Lord was so
sickened by human wickedness that *"it repented the Lord that he had
made man on the earth, and it grieved him at his heart" (Gn 6:6).* In
Genesis 7:6 God said, *"I will destroy man whom I have created from the
face of the earth; both man, and beast, and the creeping thing, and the
fowls of the air; for it repenteth me that I have made them."* Sin had en-
veloped the human race. Although God had foreknowledge mankind
would reject living for Him, their choices still greatly grieved Him.

There was but one man in this vast ocean of evil men whose life stood out like a bright light against the darkness of sinful mankind.

This man was Noah. *Genesis* 6:8 reads, *"But Noah found grace in the eyes of the Lord."* He found grace because he rejected an immoral, sinful lifestyle and pursued living righteously before God. The Scriptures tell us that Noah was a preacher of righteousness (2 Pt 2:5). Noah encouraged his fellow man to turn away from their lifestyle of sin and begin living morally right before their Creator God. He warned his generation if they rejected God they would be destroyed. Sadly, not one person heeded Noah's warnings. Instead, humanity continued to live in rebellion against God.

Due to man's sin, God destroyed everything He created through a world-wide flood annihilating all land animals and human life. The Lord was merciful however and spared Noah, his wife, his three sons, and their wives. Eight people in all were saved from God's judgment of sin through a massive Ark God had instructed Noah to build. At this point in history, the earth's population had multiplied exponentially from the days of Cain and Able.[47] Research has shown there could have been at least one billion people living on the earth during the time of Noah.[48] If that estimate is true, then that means that 99.99+ percent of the people on earth hated God and His standard for living.

God spoke to Noah about his plan to judge sin with a flood when Noah was around 500 years old. He also revealed to Noah His plan of rescue for Noah and his family (Gn 5:32). The Lord gave Noah 100 years notice about the flood to come, giving him ample time to build the great Ark (Gn 5:32; 7:6). God provided Noah with specific building instructions (Gn 6:14-16). Unfortunately, Noah's Ark is often depicted in our modern world as a child's cartoon or as a toy with 10 or 15 animals squished into a disproportioned little boat. **Quite the contrary to the cartoonish image sold to the public, Noah's Ark was designed to perfection for floating, even on the roughest of sea storms.** Did you know that the design of Noah's Ark is so perfectly stable that engineers use similar dimensions for ships today!?[49] After construction was complete, Noah and his seven family members entered the massive floating vessel as God commanded. They did not enter alone however! God commanded Noah to bring animals into the boat with them. The Lord did so for three reasons: repopulation, sacrifices, and food.

The first reason animals were to be brought on the Ark was for repopulation after the flood.

> *But with thee will I establish my covenant; and thou shalt come into the ark, thou, and thy sons, and thy wife, and thy sons' wives with thee. And of every living thing of all flesh, two of every sort shalt thou bring into the ark, to keep them alive with thee; they shall be male and female. Of fowls after their kind, and of cattle after their kind, of every creeping thing of the earth after his kind, two of every sort shall come unto thee, to keep them alive. And take thou unto thee of all food that is eaten, and thou shalt gather it to thee; and it shall be for food for thee, and for them.*

Genesis 6:18-21

In this text God instructed Noah to bring two of every kind of animal in the world onto the Ark. Of course, animals that lived in the water wouldn't need to be brought on the boat since they could live in the flood waters to come! Each pair of land animals that entered the Ark were male and female. Noah and his family were charged with keeping and feeding all the animals so the animals could reproduce after the flood waters were gone.

The second reason animals were to be brought on the Ark was for sacrifices. God commanded Noah to bring seven pairs of *clean* animals onto the Ark for sacrifices. The Scripture reads, *"Of every clean beast thou shalt take to thee by sevens, the male and his female: and of beasts that are not clean by two, the male and his female" (Gn 7:2-3).* In this passage we learn there are such things as *clean* and *unclean* animals. If you recall, Cain and Abel were required by God to offer a blood sacrifice for their sins. An offering of blood is the only atonement God recognizes as a covering for sin which is one reason why Cain's offering was not good enough and rejected by God. Later God talks to a man named Moses about blood sacrifices and clean and unclean animals in greater detail, but for now we see that from Adam to Noah people were aware that sacrifices needed to be made and there was a distinction between clean and unclean animals. In this verse, we see Noah was to bring both clean and unclean animals with him on the Ark. Both clean and unclean animals were brought to repopulate the world after it was wiped clear of all life on land, but the clean animals had a special use for sacrifices and later for food, which meant there needed to be more of them.

The third reason animals were to be brought on the Ark was for food. Many Bible scholars believe both people and animals were vegetarians prior to Noah's flood.[50] Their deduction is made from two main passages of Scripture. The first passage is from the creation week found in *Genesis 1:29*, which states, *"And God said, Behold, I have given you every herb bearing seed, which is upon the face of all the earth, and every tree, in the which is the fruit of a tree yielding seed; to you it shall be for meat [food]."*[51] The second passage comes just after the flood recedes, when God confirms His covenant with Noah. The passage reads,

> *And God blessed Noah and his sons, and said unto them,*
> *Be fruitful, and multiply, and replenish the earth. And the*
> *fear of you and the dread of you shall be upon every*
> *beast of the earth, and upon every fowl of the air, upon*
> *all that moveth upon the earth, and upon all the fishes of*
> *the sea; into your hand are they delivered. Every moving*

*thing that liveth shall be meat for you; even as the green
herb have I given you all things.*

Genesis 9:1-3

These two passages indicate in the beginning God meant only plants
to be eaten for food, but after the flood God allowed animal meat to
be eaten as well. Interestingly, God did not give this command to
Noah until after he exited the Ark. So, Noah and his family would
not have eaten any animals on the Ark. We see then God perfectly
planned having additional pairs of clean animals for Noah and his
family. They would need these animals not only for sacrifice, but for
food since all the abundant vegetation the earth once held had been
destroyed in the flood. To recap, Noah brought two pairs of every
animal plus seven pairs of every clean animal, which **added up to
tons of animals (quite literally) on the Ark, and they all fit!**

Could they all fit? There are myriads of different breeds in
the animal kingdom. To think they could *all* fit on the Ark seems like
an impossible feat! However, if we look back and rewind about
4,000 years we find the animal list was not as long as it is today. In
Noah's time most of the animal breeds living today didn't even exist.
For example, he did not pack two miniature yorkies, two basset
hounds, two doberman pinchers, and two of *every* dog breed onto
the Ark. They didn't exist! No, he simply brought a male and female
representative of the original dog kind, and did the same with the
rest of the land animals. This would bring down the animal count
considerably, making it entirely possible for all the animals to fit! In
fact, creation scientists believe there were about 16,000 animals living on the Ark with Noah and his family.[52] (Check out Fig. 2.1 for a
conception drawing of what the great Ark may have looked like.)

Having this new paradigm, it is much easier to grasp how all
the land animals fit on Noah's Ark. The following excerpt was written by creation scientist, John Woodmorappe.

According to the Bible, the ark had three decks
(floors). It is not difficult to show that there was
plenty of room for 16,000 animals, assuming they
required approximately the same floor space as
animals in typical farm enclosures and laboratories
today. The vast majority of the creatures (birds, rep-
tiles, and mammals) are small. The largest animals
were probably only a few hundred pounds of body
weight.[53]

Noah's Ark Conception Drawing

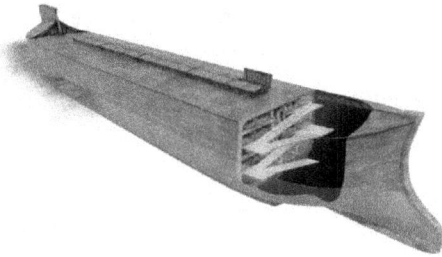

Fig. 2.1: A conception drawing of Noah's Ark from answersingensis.org.[54]

To the surprise of many skeptics, all the land animals fit just fine on
Noah's Ark with plenty of room to spare!

The Ark was finally completed after Noah and his family
labored long and diligently over the years. The time had come to at
last enter this massive vessel. After the family and all the animals
had boarded safely, God did a powerful thing. *Genesis* 7:16 reads,
*"And they that went in, went in male and female of all flesh, as God had
commanded him: and the Lord shut him in."* **God Himself shut the
door! He sealed in those who obeyed Him, and shut out
those who had rejected Him.** Judgement is a topic our modern
world regularly avoids. However, where sin is present judgement is
sure to follow. **The story of the flood is a story of sin and
judgement, but also of God's mercy and salvation to those
who obey Him.** The people on earth had been deliberately com-

mitting vile sins against God and it grieved Him deeply. There came a point when He needed to administer justice to save mankind from utter wickedness. When God shut the door of the Ark, His righteous judgment had begun. The obedient were sealed inside safe from judgement, and those who had not repented were locked outside to face the penalty for their sins.

The great waters of world judgment God had warned about beat and smote earth with a reckoning blow, forever changing the face of earth. It was as if the waters were wiping clean earth's slate, allowing God to begin again. At this time Noah was 600 years old (Gn 7:11). The great flood waters overcame the earth from two places: the sky and the ground. From above, God poured down a continual rainfall upon earth for 40 days and nights. From beneath, God cracked open earth's surface and unleashed the underground waters spilling out flood torrents making this the greatest deluge the world will ever see. The combination of waters from above and beneath engulfed the entire earth. The Bible even says that *"the mountains were covered" (Gn 7:20)*. Can you imagine what Noah and his family were experiencing on the Ark? The world they knew was gone. Every person they had known had been executed by the Lord. God's judgement is serious. Science confirms Noah's flood. There are numerous scientific evidences that can be examined today. One of the clearest pieces of evidence is the abundance of sea life unearthed from the most unusual areas. Seashells are found on mountain peaks all over the world and large water mammal bones in the middle of the desert![55] These examples and many more archeological evidences confirm the truth of the world-wide flood Noah's family was saved from because of God's abundant grace on their lives. **He could've wiped out mankind altogether, but His just judgment is always paired with great mercy and He gave mankind another chance to seek His heart and ways.**

The story of Noah is an incredible part of our history reminding us of God's judgement towards man's sin and His mercy for those who obey Him. God chose to bring a world-wide flood on earth to cleanse it from the wickedness of man, while designing a lifesaving plan for those who truly love and seek after His ways. Unfortunately, not long after the water receded from the flooded earth, Noah's descendants began to willfully reject God's Word and the sinfulness of man continued.

Babel

The flood waters receded and the eight people, along with all the animals, stepped onto dry ground for the first time after being aboard the Ark for over a year! God then instructed them accordingly, *"Be fruitful, and multiply, and replenish the earth" (Gn 9:1).* Noah's sons were fruitful, multiplying abundantly! *Genesis* 10 records Noah's lineage through his three sons. In chapter 11 the Scripture records how Noah's descendants turned and rebelled against God's command through the historical account of the Tower of Babel. This story of Babel is vital in understanding how man's sin continued after the flood. There were two specific areas where man rebelled against God during that time.

First, the people rebelled against God's command given in the ninth chapter of *Genesis*, which reads, *"And God blessed Noah and his sons, and said unto them, Be fruitful, and multiply, and replenish the earth" (Gn 9:1).* Noah's descendants were partially faithful in obeying the Lord through being fruitful and multiplying, but they did not *fully* obey. The area of their disobedience is found in the last part of the verse, *"replenish the earth".* This phrase meant God wanted the people to *fill* the earth. Instead of filling earth the people remained together. The first four verses of *Genesis* 11 paint a clear picture of the scene. The text reads,

And the whole earth was of one language, and of one speech. And it came to pass, as they journeyed from the east, that they found a plain in the land of Shinar; and they dwelt there. And they said one to another, Go to, let us make brick, and burn them thoroughly. And they had brick for stone, and slime had they for morter. And they said, Go to, let us build us a city and a tower, whose top may reach unto heaven; and let us make us a name, lest we be scattered abroad upon the face of the whole earth.

Genesis 11:1-4

After the flood the people purposely chose to disobey The Lord's instruction to fill the earth. Instead, they chose to congregate together. When the people rejected God's command to fill up the earth, it caused them to fall in yet another area.

Secondly, the people sinned in being prideful. As *Genesis* 11:1-4 highlights, the people desired to build a tower whose top might reach into heaven to make a name for themselves. They wanted a reputation or fame for their great tower. In short, they were filled with pride at their engineering knowledge, and desired to build a tower, not for the glory of God, but for their *own* glory. The Bible speaks often about pride. The word pride occurs 49 times throughout the 66 books of the KJV Bible. For instance, the Bible says, *"Pride goeth before destruction, And an haughty spirit before a fall" (Pr 18:16).* Another proverb says, *"A man's pride shall bring him low: But honour shall uphold the humble in spirit" (Pr 29:23).* The Apostle John wrote about pride, as well. He said, *"For all that is in the world, the lust of the flesh, and the lust of the eyes, and the pride of life, is not of the Father, but is of the world" (1 Jn 2:16).* Pride has been the downfall of many people in this world. The Bible also teaches pride was the sin that caused Satan's fall (Is 14:12-15). As was already referenced, Satan was originally created as an angel in the Kingdom of Heaven. Satan's angelic name was Lucifer. The Bible says that Lucifer was beautiful (Ez 28:12-14). But, Lucifer became puffed up with a mounting, dreadful pride, and God in His holy judgement cast him from heaven without a chance of redemption (Is 14:12-15; Lk 10:18; Re 20:10). This angel was the first of God's creation to fall into the trap of pride. Lucifer was brought down with pride, and its deceitfulness still seduces many today. **Pride is the root of all sin, and we should make haste to distance ourselves from it.**

The people's rebellion against God in not spreading out and filling the earth along with their sin of desiring to build a tower of pride brought judgement from God. In *Genesis* 11 the Bible explains how God dealt with these sins. The judgement He chose also answers two questions raised by historians today: One, where did all of the languages in the world come from? Two, where did all of the different "races" in the world come from? The Scripture reads,

> *And the Lord came down to see the city and the tower, which the children of men builded. And the Lord said, Behold, the people is one, and they have all one language; and this they begin to do: and now nothing will be restrained from them, which they have imagined to do. Go to, let us go down, and there confound their language, that they may not understand one another's speech. So the Lord scattered them abroad from thence upon the face of all the earth: and they left off to build the city. Therefore is the name of it called Babel; because the Lord did there confound the language of all the earth: and from thence did the Lord scatter them abroad upon the face of all the earth.*
>
> *Genesis 11:5-9*

Man had sinned yet again and God saw it, for nothing is hidden from His sight. God executed His judgement upon the people by smiting their language, which instantly caused them to fulfill His will. No more were they all of one tongue and able to understand each other. Now they had various languages and through this God caused them to scatter throughout the world separating them by their speech. Also at that time there was no such thing as "races." In reality, even today **there is only one "race," the human race. The Bible teaches all people are descendants from Adam and Eve (Acts 17:26).** "Races" have been created in the minds of men. All people are one race, despite the differences in skin tone. Truly, the differences in skin tone can be easily explained scientifically based upon the genetic code. The following excerpt from the experts at *Answers In Genesis* will help provide a good summary of how our genes produce different skin shades.

> Skin shade is governed by multiple genes and is quite complex, but for the sake of simplicity, assume for a moment that there are only two. Genes come in pairs of pairs. During reproduction, half of the genes passed on to the offspring come from each parent. For this discussion, let's assign the letters "A" and "B" to the genes that code for large amounts of melanin—the brown-colored pigment in everyone's skin. We'll also use the letters "a" and "b" to designate the genes for small amounts of melanin.
>
> In very dark-skinned people groups, individuals carry AABB genes and only produce dark-skinned offspring. In very light-skinned people groups, individuals carry aabb genes and only produce light-skinned offspring.
>
> If a male and female from each group mate and produce a child, the combination of their AABB and aabb genes would give rise to a child who carries the AaBb genes for melanin and would be "middle brown" in skin shade. Now, if two people carrying the AaBb genes got married and reproduced, their children could have a wide rage of skin colors.
>
> If Adam and Eve were both middle brown (AaBb), they would have produced children with a wide range of tones. Suddenly, all of us being one race doesn't seem so complicated.[56]

As you can see, regardless of the differences in skin color, science confirms all people are one race! After God scattered the people throughout the earth, the gene pool became isolated within

the distinct language groups God put them into. The Lord's actions
resulted in "less genetic variability" among the people groups.[57] The
genetics of each group became distinct and resulted in the variety of
skin tones represented on the earth today. God views people of all
skin colors as equal. We are all His children. Just like skin tone,
other physical characteristics are a result of Adam and Eve's genetic
variation.[58] After God scattered the people, not only did skin tones
attain dominance, but other characteristics as well, such as eye
shape, nose shape, hair color, and hair texture, to name a few.

In the story of Babel we are shown how God again changed
the course of the earth due to man's sin. The Lord intervened because Noah's descendants became prideful and were not faithful in
filling the earth as He commanded. **God involves Himself in the
dealings of men because of His great love for those He created in His image and placed in His divine storyline.**

The Tower of Babel reveals the rebellious heart of man,
God's intervention, and answers two age old questions about the
origin of languages and "races". Man's sin did not cease at the Tower
of Babel, but continued amongst all people groups, and sadly plays
on in the lives of people today.

Sin & Its Consequences

The Bible teaches in *1 John* 3:4 that sin is breaking God's
law. Adam and Eve had one law and they broke it. As we will learn in
the next chapter, the Israelites had over 600 laws and they did not
obey God perfectly either. Today Christians are held accountable to
moral laws God gave the Israelites. (We will look closer at this in the
fifth chapter on The Church.) When Adam and Eve broke God's law
they brought a curse from God upon themselves and all humanity.
Death was the punishment for breaking God's law. Death meant two
things. One, all people would die physically. Two, Adam, Eve and all

people would now be spiritually dead (Gn 2:17; 2 Th 1:7-9). The
beautiful relationship they shared with their Creator had been destroyed. God is perfect. He can not have fellowship with anyone who
rejects His holy, loving leadership. **Due to God's infinite love
and righteous justice, He must punish each lawbreaker.**

To help you understand God's justice better, think about
what happens when man breaks man's law. He pays man's fine,
right? Indeed, he does. In the same way, when man breaks God's
law, he pays God's fine. The problem was and still is that man is unable to pay God's fine. God's standard is perfection. Both the Old
and New Testaments teach that due to our sinful nature we are unable to keep God's law perfectly. The Bible says, *"All have sinned"*
(Rm 3:23). Humanity has been and is (to use the old cliche) between
a rock and a hard place. Every person has broken God's law and
must pay the fine. Only, we are unable to pay the fine. Therefore, we
must experience God's sentence of just judgement. Throughout the
Bible we learn more about God's justice. God's justice for sinful man
is an eternal prison. This prison is often called hell, or the lake of
fire. Hell is a real place and those who haven't paid the fine for their
sins will go there. Thankfully, God has made a way for man to "pay
his fine" and restore his broken relationship with his Creator and
escape the judgement to come. It is wonderful Good News, but since
that marvelous news is the first climax of God's story we are going to
wait until chapter four to unveil this hope-filled plan!

In the beginning, God taught Adam and Eve what was right
and wrong. Even though the people knew right from wrong, as we
have seen in this chapter, many chose to sin against the Lord. After
the dispersion at Babel God set about to form a nation for Himself;
A nation He would communicate with; A people who would know
His laws because He would instruct them to write them down and
teach them to each other. God would reveal Himself to this nation

unlike He had done with any other people on the face of the earth. This nation is Israel.

Chapter Three

ISRAEL

"I am the Lord, your Holy One, the creator of Israel, your King... This people have I formed for myself; they shall shew [show] forth my praise."

Isaiah 43:15; 21

The Story Line

Two thousand and forty nine years after the creation of the heavens and the earth, God's man, Abraham, came into the picture. God chose Abraham and His descendants to build a nation, a people, whom He would reveal Himself to, so they would obey Him and inform the world about the truth of God. The Israelite's were unique in all the earth, they were the only nation God formed to reveal Himself to so one day He could make Himself known to every person He created!

Abraham, Isaac, & Jacob

Abraham

Eight generations after Noah's Ark landed, a man named Terah, a descendant of Shem (one of Noah's three sons), became the father of Abram, Nahor, and Haran. This family lived in Ur of the Chaldeans, which is modern day eastern Iraq. After Terah died, The Lord spoke to Abram saying,

> *Get thee out of thy country, and from thy kindred, and from thy father's house, unto a land that I will shew [show] thee: And I will make of thee a great nation, and I will bless thee, and make thy name great; and thou shalt be a blessing: And I will bless them that bless thee, and curse him that curseth thee: and in thee shall all families of the earth be blessed.*

Genesis 12:1-3

Abram obeyed God. He left with his wife, his nephew, and all the wealth he had accumulated-his livestock and all the people he had taken into his household, and headed west for the land of Canaan (Gn 12:5). Abram gave up all he had known to follow God. Traveling west, Abram needed plenty of land and water to nourish the people who journeyed with him and their animals. He trekked up and down the eastern Mediterranean Sea faithfully searching and listening for God's guidance. During Abram's travels he faced many challenges but he continued to follow the Lord.

In *Genesis* 15, God made a covenant with Abram. A covenant is a legally binding contract. (For more information about covenants please read Appendix I on page 198.) The covenantal text reads:

> *After these things the word of the Lord came unto Abram in a vision, saying, Fear not, Abram: I am thy shield, and thy exceeding great reward. And Abram said, Lord God, what wilt thou give me, seeing I go childless, and the steward of my house is this Eliezer of Damascus? And*

Abram said, Behold, to me thou hast given no seed: and, lo, one born in my house is mine heir. And, behold, the word of the Lord came unto him, saying, This shall not be thine heir; but he that shall come forth out of thine own bowels shall be thine heir. And he brought him forth abroad, and said, Look now toward heaven, and tell the stars, if thou be able to number them: and he said unto him, So shall thy seed be. And he believed in the Lord; and he counted it to him for righteousness.

Genesis 15:1-6

God first spoke to Abram in chapter 12 telling him to leave his homeland for The Lord was going to make him into a great nation. Abram was obedient to the Lord in leaving his homeland, but he and his wife, Sari, were not conceiving a son. Both Abram and his wife were getting old and Sari was past the age of childbearing (Gn 18:11). The Scriptures tell us Abram was puzzled at how God would fulfill His Words. This short dialogue between he and The Lord shows Abram thought his servant, Eliezer of Damascus, would have to be his heir since he had no son. The Lord explained to Abram he *would* have a son. One night, God called Abram outside his tent and brought his attention to the countless stars visible in the vast countryside. Then The Lord said, *"So shall thy seed be" (Gn 15:5).* So shall thy seed be!? Wow! God was telling Abram his descendants would be countless like the stars in the night sky! God's Words removed all doubt from Abram's mind. Once Abram was reassured by God he would conceive a son, the Scriptures record one of the most important verses in the Bible in *Genesis* 15:6, which reads *"And he [Abram] believed in the Lord; and he counted it to him for righteousness."* Because of Abram's belief (faith) in God's Word, The Lord counted Abram as righteous. In this passage we learn **God views faith in His Word as the cornerstone of being righteous in His eyes.** This is extremely important, because it's the first time in the Bible the word *believe* is mentioned. Abram is the forefather of all who believe in God by faith. **Faith is having confidence God will fulfill His**

Word, even when one can't understand how that may be
(Hb 11:1). (Faith will be discussed in greater detail in Chapter Five.)
It wasn't long until God's promise to Abram came to pass. Abram
and his wife, Sari, miraculously conceived a son in their old age. The
boy's name was Isaac.

After Isaac's birth, God reaffirmed his covenant with
Abram. God then changed Abram and Sari's name to Abraham and
Sarah. God also gave Abraham a sign of the covenant He had made
with him, which was circumcision. Abraham and all the males in his
household, born or purchased, were required to be circumcised as a
sign they were partaking in the covenant God gave Abraham regarding the land of Canaan (Gn 17). Years passed and Abraham took
much pleasure in his son Isaac! As any good papa would, Abraham
probably delighted in teaching his boy many things. When Isaac was
about 10 years old the Lord God once again spoke to Abraham, but
this time His message was different. God's Words to Abraham are
found in *Genesis* 22:1-2:

> *And it came to pass after these things, that God did tempt*
> *Abraham, and said unto him, Abraham: and he said,*
> *Behold, here I am. And he said, Take now thy son, thine*
> *only son Isaac, whom thou lovest, and get thee into the*
> *land of Moriah; and offer him there for a burnt offering*
> *upon one of the mountains which I will tell thee of.*

Hold on one second! What is God asking Abraham to do? God
commands Abraham to take his son Isaac, his *only* son, and sacrifice
him as a burnt offering, What!? At first this command seems impossible, but God isn't tempting Abraham to do evil, rather, He is putting Abraham in a situation where his faith will be proved[59] (Ja
1:13). There is a purpose behind this command which unfolds
throughout the rest of the chapter. But first, the phrase *"thine only*
son Isaac" needs to be highlighted. As you read through the book of
Genesis you'll find Abraham had another son first, but that child

was not the child of the promise, the miracle child. Abraham's first son was born through human effort from Sarah's maidservant. Whereas, Isaac was brought about by the miraculous working of the Lord Almighty. God did not view Abraham's first child the same as He did Isaac, since Isaac was of supernatural descent and the one whom He would fulfill His promises through. Though Abraham loved both children, his wife Sarah did not care for the maidservant's first born because he picked on her son, Isaac. The bullying actions of the first born caused he and his mother to be banished from Abraham's household and their community.

So we see Isaac is special to both God and Abraham. And now God wants Abraham to sacrifice him?! In obedience, Abraham journeyed for three days taking with him two of his servants and Isaac, his beloved son. Upon reaching their destination, Abraham begins to display his faith by saying to his servants, *"Abide ye here with the ass [donkey]; and I and the lad will go yonder and worship, and come again to you" (Gn 22:5).* Did you catch that!? Remember, Abraham has been instructed by God to sacrifice his son Isaac, yet, Abraham informs his servants he *and the boy* will return! Abraham's words proved he had confidence God was going to intervene in some fashion. He knew this to be true based upon the covenant God had made with him. God had promised to Abraham his descendants would be as numerous as the stars in the sky. The only way this could happen was if Isaac, his son, his only son, would live. Abraham's words to his servants indicated he believed God would either prevent him from going through with the sacrifice or God would raise Isaac from the dead. Either way, Abraham is demonstrating his faith in God's covenant is firm. Leaving the servants behind, father and son journeyed further and the Bible records the story in the following words:

> *And they came to the place which God had told him of;*
> *and Abraham built an altar there, and laid the wood in*

*order, and bound Isaac his son, and laid him on the altar
upon the wood. And Abraham stretched forth his hand,
and took the knife to slay his son. And the angel of the
Lord called unto him out of heaven, and said, Abraham,
Abraham: and he said, Here am I. And he said, Lay not
thine hand upon the lad, neither do thou any thing unto
him: for now I know that thou fearest God, seeing thou
hast not withheld thy son, thine only son from me. And
Abraham lifted up his eyes, and looked, and behold behind him a ram caught in a thicket by his horns: and
Abraham went and took the ram, and offered him up for
a burnt offering in the stead of his son. And Abraham
called the name of that place Jehovahjireh: as it is said
to this day, In the mount of the Lord it shall be seen. And
the angel of the Lord called unto Abraham out of heaven
the second time, And said, By myself have I sworn, saith
the Lord, for because thou hast done this thing, and hast
not withheld thy son, thine only son: That in blessing I
will bless thee, and in multiplying I will multiply thy seed
as the stars of the heaven, and as the sand which is upon
the sea shore; and thy seed shall possess the gate of his
enemies; And in thy seed shall all the nations of the earth
be blessed; because thou hast obeyed my voice. So Abraham returned unto his young men, and they rose up and
went together to Beersheba; and Abraham dwelt at Beersheba.*

Genesis 22:9-19

This was a significant, pivotal test the Lord put to Abraham, and his faith proved solid and true in the Lord his God. This passage of Scripture not only confirms Abraham's faith, but also is a symbolic picture of the salvation story we learn more about in the next chapter of this book.

Throughout Abraham's life his faith in God seemed to grow stronger and stronger. When God spoke to Abraham the first time, Abraham in faith left all he had known to go to a land God would show him. Abraham again had faith he and Sarah would conceive a child in their old age, even though it took a miracle. Then, Abraham displayed faith believing somehow, someway, God would keep Isaac alive, despite God's directions for the sacrifice. He followed the Lord's instructions even when it seemed to man's logic the effect would destroy the future of his descendants and God's covenant. Abraham is a man of great faith, and rightly so, given he is the father of the nation of Israel.

Surprisingly, Abraham was blessed with more sons after Isaac, but Isaac was the son of God's promise. He was the miracle child (Gn 22:2). God next reveals Himself to Isaac, in whom He continues to fulfill His covenant promise to build a nation unto Himself.

Isaac

Abraham passed on into eternity and Isaac grew into a man. The Lord chose to reaffirm His covenant with Abraham's son, Isaac, as a severe famine afflicted Canaan, the promised land of the covenant. The Scriptures read,

And the Lord appeared unto him [Isaac], and said, Go not down into Egypt; dwell in the land which I shall tell thee of: Sojourn in this land, and I will be with thee, and will bless thee; for unto thee, and unto thy seed, I will give all these countries, and I will perform the oath which I sware [swore] unto Abraham thy father; And I will make thy seed to multiply as the stars of heaven, and will give unto thy seed all these countries; and in thy seed shall all the nations of the earth be blessed; Because that Abraham obeyed my voice, and kept my charge, my commandments, my statutes, and my laws. And Isaac dwelt in Gerar:

Genesis 26:2-6

God is now informing Isaac, the child of God's promise, his descendants would be given possession of all the countries which make up the land of Canaan. God also makes clear He is doing so because Isaac's father, Abraham, obeyed God. Like his father, Isaac faced many challenges throughout his life, especially with his neighbors who occupied the promised land. They viewed him as they did

Abraham, a foreigner, which is why they called them *Hebrews*, which means "from the other side."[60] Although God promised this land to Isaac's descendants, *he* was the foreigner in the land. Despite his neighbor's hostility towards his presence, Isaac was abundantly prosperous with God's blessing. The Bible says in *Genesis* 26 Isaac reaped one hundred times the seed he planted. He was also wealthy in animals and servants. Isaac's Philistine neighbors grew exceedingly envious. They attempted to disrupt Isaac's prosperity and drive him away by filling up the wells his father had dug, one after the other. After a handful of disputes over the wells, Isaac decided to dig a new well and finally found peace in the land. He then settled in Beersheba, where the Lord appeared and spoke to him saying, *"I am the God of Abraham thy father: fear not, for I am with thee, and will bless thee, and multiply thy seed for my servant Abraham's sake" (Gn 26:24).* Just like He did for Abraham, God is reaffirming His promise to Isaac later in his life.

Isaac was 60 years old when he and his wife, Rebekah, had twin boys, Jacob and Esau (Gn 25:26). During Rebekah's pregnancy, the Bible recounts the twins *"struggled within her" (Gn 25:22).* So great was their struggle it caused her to inquire of the Lord why it was so. The Lord gave her this answer, *"Two nations are in thy womb, and two manner of people shall be separated from thy bowels; and the one people shall be stronger than the other people; and the elder shall serve the younger" (Gn 25:23).* When the boys were born Esau came out first, and then Jacob holding onto his brother's heel. The boys grew up and had different interests. Esau enjoyed the outdoors and hunting, while Jacob enjoyed the home life where it was more peaceful and quiet. Their differing personalities caused Isaac to favor Esau and Rebekah to favor Jacob. Back in these days the order of birth was very significant. The firstborn son would receive a special inheritance of his father's wealth, because it would most likely be his responsibility to take care of his mother and remaining household when his father passed away.[61] Since Esau was the firstborn, custom designated he had these rights. The Bible reveals to us, however, Esau did not value his God-given birthright. The story begins with Esau coming in from a day of hunting, weary from exceeding hunger.

> Esau said to Jacob, Feed me, I pray thee, with that same red pottage; for I am faint: therefore was his name called Edom. And Jacob said, Sell me this day thy birthright. And Esau said, Behold, I am at the point to die: and what profit shall this birthright do to me? And Jacob said, Swear to me this day; and he sware [swore] unto him: and he sold his birthright unto Jacob. Then Jacob gave Esau bread and pottage of lentils; and he did eat and drink, and rose up, and went his way: thus Esau despised his birthright.

> *Genesis 25:30-34*

Esau was a very impulsive man, giving up his birthright for temporary gratification. He sold his inheritance, position, and responsibility of the eldest brother for a bowl of soup! Esau's hasty actions display he had no regard for his family obligation. As Isaac grew older the story of Jacob and Esau gets even more intriguing.

Genesis 27 records the story of Isaac passing on the Abrahamic blessing to one of his sons. In Abraham's life, Isaac was chosen to carry on the covenant God made with Abraham. God then chose only one of Isaac's sons to carry on the covenant blessing. Since Esau was the first born and his father favored him, Isaac intended to give this son his blessing. Rebekah, on the other hand, favored Jacob. She decided to intervene and take matters into her own hands, justifying her actions by recalling God's Words when the twins were in her womb, *"...and the elder shall serve the younger" (Gn 25:23)*. When the time came for Isaac to pass on the blessing he called for Esau. Isaac had grown very old and believed his time on earth was growing short. He asked Esau to cook him his favorite meal and afterwards would give him his blessing. When Isaac and Esau were talking, Rebekah eavesdropped on their conversation. As soon as Esau left to hunt wild game for the meal, his mother informed Jacob of her husband's plan to bless Esau. Quickly, Rebekah directed Jacob to pretend he was Esau so as to deceive his papa into giving *him* the covenant blessing. The scene was tense! Isaac's old age had brought with it poor and failing eyesight which caused Jacob's impersonation of Esau to be successful! Reading the account yourself in the Bible you will see Jacob quite literally "pulled the wool over Isaac's eyes!" Convinced Jacob was Esau, Isaac proceeded to speak forth his blessing over Jacob. The words of blessing were,

> *Therefore God give thee of the dew of heaven, and the fatness of the earth, and plenty of corn and wine: Let people serve thee, and nations bow down to thee: be lord over thy brethren, and let thy mother's sons bow down to thee: cursed be every one that curseth thee, and blessed be he that blesseth thee... And God Almighty bless thee, and make thee fruitful, and multiply thee, that thou mayest be a multitude of people; And give thee the blessing of Abraham, to thee, and to thy seed with thee; that thou mayest inherit the land wherein thou art a stranger, which God gave unto Abraham.*

Genesis 27:28-29; 28:3-4

When Isaac spoke these words he was passing the covenant God had made with Abraham on to Jacob and God's blessing would continue through *his* lineage. Little did Isaac know he was fulfilling the words God spoke to Rebecca years ago (Gn 25:23). Once the blessing had been spoken Jacob left Isaac's presence, and Esau soon returned with meat and excitement to receive his father's blessing! Isaac discovered he had been deceived by Jacob, but he knew his words could not be retracted. Esau deeply mourned at the loss of his blessing and begged his father for one, but Isaac declared there was no blessing left for him... it had all been given to Jacob.

Jacob

After Jacob had been given the blessing by his father, Esau was enraged and planned to kill him. Rebecca urged Jacob to flee and live with her brother, Laban. Jacob obeyed and left for his Uncle's home. Laban received his nephew with open arms, promptly putting him to work, and it wasn't long before Laban's daughter, Rachel, caught Jacob's eye. Jacob told Laban he would work for him seven years if he would give him his daughter's hand in marriage. Laban said, "Yes!" filling Jacob's heart with great joy! Although seven years is a long time, the Bible records that these years *"seemed unto him but a few days, for the love he had for her" (Gn 29:20).* After the seven years had been fulfilled Laban hosted the wedding party for his daughter and Jacob. That evening they came together as husband and wife to celebrate their marriage. In the morning Jacob woke up with the shocking discovery that the woman he loved and worked seven years to marry was not his wife! He had been tricked into marrying Leah, Rachel's sister! Jacob confronted Laban, demanding to know why he had been deceived with Leah when he had worked seven years for Rachel! His Uncle responded saying, *"It must not be so done in our country, to give the younger before the firstborn. Fulfil her week, and we will give thee this also for the service which thou shalt serve with me yet seven other years" (Gn 29:26-27).* So after a week of marriage to Leah and a commitment to work another seven years, Jacob was given Rachel, his true love, to marry. During that time in history marrying more than one wife was common, for through each wife a man could have more children and children resulted in a large family with many hands that could work. Having more than one spouse is not the biblical model. God intended one man to be with one woman, however because of man's sinful nature, people often transgressed in this area. Also during this time era, wealthy women generally possessed a maid, a "young unmarried woman, often of the servant class."[62] Both Rachel and Leah had a maid and they became a big part of the story of Jacob and the nation of Israel.

The Bible tells us Jacob did not love Leah. The Lord saw Jacob's hatred for Leah and so blessed her with children, but Rachel was unable to conceive. After Leah gave birth to Reuben, Simeon, Levi, and Judah, Rachel became exceedingly jealous and could not endure her barrenness any longer! She gave her maid, Bilhah, to Jacob so he would have children through her on Rachel's behalf. Jacob obliged her and Bilhah bore him two sons, Dan and Naphtali. Then Leah became jealous because she wasn't having any more children so she gave her maid, Zilpah, to Jacob as well to bear additional children for her. Zilpah gave Jacob two more sons, Gad and Asher. Later, Leah surprisingly found herself pregnant again and bore Jacob two additional sons, Issachar and Zebulun. Finally after years of waiting, God blessed Rachel's barren womb with two boys, Joseph and later Benjamin. These four women bore Jacob twelve sons, who played a critical role in God's divine storyline. After Jacob completed his 14 years of service to Laban for his two wives, he desired to take all God had bestowed him with and return to his own country.

Jacob gathered up his household and possessions and left his Uncle's land. Not long after this Jacob encountered the Lord in a most unusual way. In *Genesis* 32 the Bible tells us Jacob wrestled with God! You may ask, How is this possible? The Old Testament records a few times how God took on the appearance of a man. He did so with Adam and Eve in the Garden of Eden, with Abraham, and here again with Jacob. The God-man pictured in these events throughout Scripture is referred to as the pre-incarnate Christ. That is, Jesus (God) walking as a man on earth prior to His birth into the world. In these instances, **The Lord miraculously walks onto the scene of His story in human form.** The following text clearly records Jacob saw God face to face, at least God's veiled glory in a human body:

> And Jacob was left alone; and there wrestled a man with him until the breaking of the day. And when he saw that he prevailed not against him, he touched the hollow of his thigh; and the hollow of Jacob's thigh was out of joint, as he wrestled with him. And he said, Let me go, for the day breaketh. And he said, I will not let thee go, except thou bless me. And he said unto him, What is thy name? And he said, Jacob. And he said, Thy name shall be called no more Jacob, but Israel: for as a prince hast thou power with God and with men, and hast prevailed. And Jacob asked him, and said, Tell me, I pray thee, thy name. And he said, Wherefore is it that thou dost ask after my name? And he blessed him there. And Jacob called the name of the place Peniel: for I have seen God face to face, and my life is preserved.

Genesis 32:24-30

This wrestling match dramatically changed Jacob's future and that of the whole world! Jacob and the pre-incarnate Christ wrestled through the night. Why? They seem to have wrestled for the purpose of testing Jacob, whether or not he truly desired to be blessed by God. Because Jacob was unwaveringly determined to be blessed by this man whom he knew was divine, God gave him his desire. His blessing was threefold. First, God changed Jacob's name to Israel which means "one who fights victoriously with God" or "a prevailing prince with God." [63] In other words, it seems God was telling Jacob he and his descendants were chosen to fight for righteousness on the earth. Next, God revealed to Jacob he had seen God face to face and lived. Lastly, God gave Jacob a bittersweet blessing in injuring Jacob's hip. This injury caused him a life-long limp, which was a constant reminder of this wrestling match that Jacob would never forget, possibly so he would always keep focused on God.

God changed Jacob's name to *Israel!* Israel was the nation God had promised to Abraham in *Genesis* 12:2-3 in which God said, *"I will make of thee a great nation, and I will bless thee, and make thy name great; and thou shalt be a blessing: And I will bless them that bless thee, and curse him that curseth thee: and in thee shall all families of the earth be blessed."* This promise was not fulfilled immediately, but became more substantially visible through Abraham's grandson, Jacob. The name Israel is extremely important in the Bible because Israel is the name of the nation God created for Himself. The nation of Israel is made up of the 12 tribes of Israel or Jacob's 12 sons: Reuben, Simeon, Levi, Judah, Dan, Naphtali, Gad, Asher, Issachar, Zebulun, Joseph, and lastly Benjamin.

Although these 12 came from a godly line of men (Abraham, Isaac, and Jacob), Israel's sons did not all follow the Lord from an early age. In fact 10 of the brothers were very jealous of Joseph, the second youngest brother born of their father's favorite wife, Rachel. Their jealousy raged so greatly they sold him into slavery. During Joseph's enslavement he was falsely charged with rape and thrown into prison. **Joseph strove to honor and please the Lord through all of his experiences and thus God's favor was with him in all he did.** God caused events to happen which resulted in Joseph's release after years in prison (Gn 41:39-46). Although multiple people had plans for evil in Joseph's life, God watched over his son. Not only was Joseph set free by the King of Egypt, but was made second in command over all of Egypt! **No person or circumstance can obstruct God's purpose for the lives of His faithful children!** The years went by and a famine struck Egypt for seven years bringing many people to the land for food, including Joseph's family. During that time Joseph and his family were reunited and reconciled through his loving forgiveness he showed them for their past wrong of selling him into slavery. Because of Joseph's high position, his family was given the best of the land where the sons of Israel prospered and multiplied greatly.

Upon the King of Egypt's death, the Bible says a new king arose who did not know Joseph. This king was concerned about how prosperous the Israelite people were growing and feared they would take over the land (Ex 1). So the kings of Egypt enslaved the Israelites. Their enslavement seemed as though the Lord had forgotten the covenant He had made with Abraham, Isaac, and Jacob, but He had not. **God had a plan for the Israelites, just as He does in your life and mine!**

Moses

Since the death of Joseph, son of Jacob, Egypt had enslaved the people of Israel out of fear they would one day overpower the Egyptians. The King of Egypt's words and actions are recorded in the first chapter *Exodus*, the second book of the Bible.

> *Behold, the people of the children of Israel are more and mightier than we: Come on, let us deal wisely with them; lest they multiply, and it come to pass, that, when there falleth out any war, they join also unto our enemies, and fight against us, and so get them up out of the land. Therefore they did set over them taskmasters to afflict them with their burdens. And they built for Pharaoh treasure cities, Pithom and Raamses. But the more they afflicted them, the more they multiplied and grew. And they were grieved because of the children of Israel.*
>
> *Exodus 1:9-12*

Even in the midst of Israel's enslavement, God blessed His people causing them to become numerous. After 300 years of slavery, the Egyptian king could no longer handle the Israelite's prosperity. So he conspired in his wicked heart an evil plan to murder all the Israelite baby boys at birth to keep the Israelite people from multiplying continually. If he could wipe out a generation of boys, he knew the future prosperity of the Israelite's would dwindle.

During this frightful and horrific time, an Israelite child named Moses was born. His mother was able to hide him for three months from the massacre of the Egyptian's atrocious edict. When she could conceal him no longer without detection, she placed her infant son inside a waterproof basket and sent him adrift down the flowing river. Baby Moses floated atop the water with God's care and direction. The Lord guided the basket and its precious cargo into a cluster of reeds near where an Egyptian princess was bathing. She spied the basket and sent her maid after it. Upon opening the basket the princess discovered the small child inside and had compassion on the crying baby. As soon as he had been rescued from the river, Moses' sister, who had followed him down the riverbank, piped up and said, *"Shall I go and call to thee a nurse of the Hebrew women, that she may nurse the child for thee" (Ex 2:7)?* The princess obliged her request! So Moses, another miracle child, was nursed by his mother until the boy was weened, and was then raised in an Egyptian palace as a prince.

Moses grew up in strength, knowledge, and power. When he had grown to be a man, he visited his people, the Hebrews, and witnessed an Egyptian beating a fellow Hebrew. The sight so greatly upset Moses he rose up to the Hebrew's defense and killed the Egyptian! Quickly, he took action and hid the dead man's body beneath the sand. On the following day, Moses went back to visit his people. This time he viewed two Hebrews fighting. He questioned them about it and one of them replied saying, *"Who made thee a prince and a judge over us? intendest thou to kill me, as thou killedst the Egyptian"* *(Ex 2:14)?* When Moses heard these words he was frightened! His actions had been found out. In fear, he ran away from Egypt to the remote desert. Moses fled and left all he had known, both his blood family and the Egyptian family who raised him. Just as the Lord had miraculously protected and provided for Moses at his birth when death should have been his fate, so also God protected and provided for him now as he was alone in the desert, away from everything he had known in Egypt.

Moses was 40 years old when he fled into the desert land of Midian and he dwelt there another 40 years. After fleeing, the Lord led Moses to a family he could reside with. As time passed Moses became part of this family's community and began a family of his own, taking a wife and having children. While Moses settled into his new life in the desert, the King of Egypt died. At that time, the Scriptures record that *"the children of Israel sighed by reason of the bondage, and they cried, and their cry came up unto God by reason of the bondage. And God heard their groaning, and God remembered his covenant with Abraham, with Isaac, and with Jacob" (Ex 2:23-24).* Then, unexpectedly, one day everything changed. Moses was going about his usual work tending his father-in-law's flock when he came upon the mountain of Sinai. On this mountain Moses heard the voice of the Lord. The Bible records Moses' startling encounter in *Exodus 3*. The following passage recounts the scene in great detail:

> *And the angel of the Lord appeared unto him [Moses] in a flame of fire out of the midst of a bush: and he looked, and, behold, the bush burned with fire, and the bush was not consumed. And Moses said, I will now turn aside, and see this great sight, why the bush is not burnt. And when the Lord saw that he turned aside to see, God called unto him out of the midst of the bush, and said, Moses, Moses. And he said, Here am I. And he said, Draw not nigh hither: put off thy shoes from off thy feet, for the place whereon thou standest is holy ground. Moreover he said, I am the God of thy father, the God of Abraham, the God of Isaac, and the God of Jacob. And Moses hid his face; for he was afraid to look upon God. And the Lord said, I have surely seen the affliction of my people which are in Egypt, and have heard their cry by reason of their taskmasters; for I know their*

sorrows; And I am come down to deliver them out of the
hand of the Egyptians, and to bring them up out of that
land unto a good land and a large, unto a land flowing
with milk and honey; unto the place of the Canaanites,
and the Hittites, and the Amorites, and the Perizzites,
and the Hivites, and the Jebusites. Now therefore, be-
hold, the cry of the children of Israel is come unto me:
and I have also seen the oppression wherewith the Egyp-
tians oppress them. Come now therefore, and I will send
thee unto Pharaoh, that thou mayest bring forth my peo-
ple the children of Israel out of Egypt.

Exodus 3:2-10

This miraculous encounter Moses had with the Lord shows God's
commitment to His promise and how He had not forgotten the
covenant He had made with Abraham. 40 years had passed since
Moses fled Egypt and left behind his own Israelite kinsman. God
was now ready to deliver His people, the Israelites, from their Egyptian bondage and bring them into the land He promised to give
them. The Lord conversed with Moses about His plans from *Exodus*
3-4:17. Their conversation is extensive and detailed and I encourage
you to read each verse. In summary, God informs Moses he is going
to be the one to bring the Israelites out of their slavery. Upon hearing this Moses protested, saying he did not feel adequately qualified.
He asked God, *"when I come unto the children of Israel, and shall say*
unto them, The God of your fathers hath sent me unto you; and they shall
say to me, What is his name? what shall I say unto them" (Ex 3:13)? God
instructed him to tell them he had been sent by *"The Lord God of your*
fathers, the God of Abraham, of Isaac, and of Jacob" (Ex 3:16). God revealed to Moses His rescue plan for His people. Moses continued to
protest that he was inadequate, but God provided him with two miraculous signs. These signs were given to Moses to show anyone who
disbelieved his words that his message was indeed from The One
True God. Moses still insisted he was not qualified, so God sent
Moses' brother, Aaron, along with Moses as a partner to free the
Israelites from their centuries long slavery. After much convincing,

Moses believed God's plan and headed toward Egypt. As he heeded the voice of the Lord, God instructed Aaron, *"Go into the wilderness to meet Moses" (Ex 5:27).* When Moses and Aaron reunited, these long lost brothers embraced with amazement and confidence in their hearts and minds at the working of God! He had brought them back together after almost 80 years of separation! Moses explained to his brother all God had told him. Then, together they made their way into Egypt and met with the elders of Israel. Upon hearing God's plan to rescue them and seeing the miracles God had given to Moses, the elders believed and worshipped the Lord (Ex 4:31)!

The Ten Plagues

Moses and Aaron encouraged the Israelites that God had heard their cries of bondage and was soon going to free them. Then they set out to ask Pharaoh to free God's people and let them go. Moses and Aaron knew their request would be denied, for the Lord had informed them ahead of time their appeal would be rejected. Their request was not only rejected, but so enraged the King of Egypt he increased the work load of the Israelite slaves as punishment. The Israelites were angrily disheartened and confronted Moses. Moses turned to the Lord and questioned God's purpose in bringing him back to Egypt to free His people when it seemed to be inflicting more evil upon them. The Lord responded to Moses by saying:

> *I am the Lord: And I appeared unto Abraham, unto Isaac, and unto Jacob, by the name of God Almighty, but by my name Jehovah was I not known to them. And I have also established my covenant with them, to give them the land of Canaan, the land of their pilgrimage, wherein they were strangers. And I have also heard the groaning of the children of Israel, whom the Egyptians keep in bondage; and I have remembered my covenant. Wherefore say unto the children of Israel, I am the Lord, and I will bring you out from under the burdens of the Egyptians, and I will rid you out of their bondage,*

and I will redeem you with a stretched out arm, and with
great judgments: And I will take you to me for a people,
and I will be to you a God: and ye shall know that I am
the Lord your God, which bringeth you out from under
the burdens of the Egyptians. And I will bring you in unto
the land, concerning the which I did swear to give it to
Abraham, to Isaac, and to Jacob; and I will give it you
for an heritage: I am the Lord.

Exodus 6:2-8

Before long, Moses and Aaron approached the King of Egypt a second time but were again refused their request. Thus, the Lord proceeded to act on the behalf of His people to show both the Egyptians and Israelites His Almighty power. God, in His unparalleled might, smote Egypt with 10 devastating plagues, one after the other, each a frightening experience. These plagues included water turning into blood, frogs, lice, flies, death of livestock, painful boils on the people, hail, locusts, utter darkness, and lastly, the death of the first born. As each plague left its scar on the Egyptians, Moses and Aaron would again and again approach the King of Egypt with their request to let God's people go, but the answer was the same, NO!

The Death of the Firstborn Plague

The last plague God brought down upon the Egyptians to show forth His might and power was the plague of death. Death would strike the first born of every household in the land of Egypt if Pharaoh would not let God's people go. However, Pharaoh's heart was hard and he did not want to give up his labor force of slaves. Pharaoh's decision unleashed God's final plague and the death angel was sent by the Lord to slay every first born in Egypt. To make a way of escape for His own people, God informed Moses what night the death angel would arrive and how the Israelites or any who believed The Lord was The One True God could spare themselves. They were to kill an unblemished lamb and paint the door posts of their home with its blood. **Anyone in a home that was covered by the**

lamb's blood would be spared. The Israelites were also to eat a special meal, called the passover meal, that God gave specific instructions for in the *Exodus* 12. This meal was called the passover, because it was to be eaten as the death angel *passed over* any home having the sign of blood on the door posts. The 10th plague was pivotal in establishing the Israelite calendar, the annual animal sacrifice, the passover meal, as well as freeing God's people from their 430 years of slavery in the land of Egypt (Ex 12).

In the night hours the chilling cries of men, women, and children rang loudly throughout the Egyptian Kingdom as one by one they discovered the deaths of their first born, from their livestock to their own children (Ex 11:6). Moses and Aaron were summoned by the king of Egypt in the middle of the night and he said unto them, *"go, serve the Lord, as ye have said. Also take your flocks and your herds, as ye have said, and be gone; and bless me also" (Ex 12:31-32).* The Egyptians lamented and mourned their dead and were terror stricken that death would overtake all of them! Thus, they pressed the Israelites to get out of Egypt quickly lest they all die! They even gave them of their riches and jewels as they began their exodus (Ex 12:33; 35-36)!

Israel's Exodus

With overwhelming joy in their hearts, the Israelites shed their chains of slavery and put on the flowing robes of freedom! The Bible tells us those leaving Egypt were *"...about six hundred thousand [Israelites] on foot that were men, beside children" (Ex 12:37).* According to *The New Defenders Study Bible,* the Israelite population at this time, including women and children, had grown to at least two million people.[64] This Israelite multitude left Egypt in its own dust and were now on their way to the land of promise led by God's own hand! The 10 plagues were over, but God's might and powerful miracles had just begun! God guided and sustained His people through the wilderness in supernatural ways! By day He led them *"...in a pillar of a cloud,..."* and by night He led them *"...in a pillar of fire, to give them light; to go by day and night" (Ex 13:21).* God performed astonishing wonders on the behalf of His people, for them and their enemies to behold. The Israelites had traveled only a short distance out of Egypt, when Pharaoh realized his slave labor was gone. His heart hardened yet again and he decided to bring them back! Mounting up the entire Egyptian army on horses and chariots, he pursued after them with a beastly fury. God had led the Israelites to the bank of the Red Sea. They soon saw the violent dust kicked up by the Egyptian army in hot pursuit after them and became panicked with fright. They came to Moses and faithlessly groaned words like, "We would be better off serving our old slave masters rather than being killed in this desolate desert" (Ex 14:12)! At these sayings, Moses uplifted the people's hearts by saying, *"Fear ye not, stand still, and see the salvation of the Lord, which he will shew [show] to you to day: for the Egyptians whom ye have seen to day, ye shall see them again no more for ever" (Ex 14:13).* **Moses rejected the critical voices which surrounded him by standing on the true words God gave him.** The Lord instructed Moses to hold up his staff and the Red Sea would miraculously part! **Moses obeyed; God moved!** The waters divided creating a path of dry ground for the Israelites to cross. All throughout the night the multitude of Israelite people crossed the sea in escape from the Egyptians, while God held their enemies back with His pillar of cloud. In the early morning hours God allowed the Egyptians to again chase after the Israelites through the Red Sea. As they pressed forward, God hindered them by ripping off their chariot wheels! At this the Egyptian's were once again awakened that God was for the Israelites and desired to retreat, but their time for judgement had come. Once the Israelites were safe on the other side, God instructed Moses to stretch out his hand over the sea to cause the water to return back into its proper place. The waters came spilling and gushing back into position, drowning the King of Egypt, his army, and all their chariots and horses. The Israelites stood on the bank witnessing God's power over their enemies and the Bible records they *"feared the Lord, and believed the Lord, and his servant Moses" (Ex 14:31).*

Israel Rejoices

The Israelites were delivered from their Egyptian oppressors and free to follow the Lord to the land promised to their forefathers, Abraham, Isaac, and Jacob. They gratefully rejoiced with a song which is recorded in *Exodus* 15. From the Red Sea God led them into the desert, but along the way they were only finding bitter water to drink. After just three days into their journey the people began to complain to Moses about the water. Moses cried out to the Lord and He provided! God told Moses to take a particular piece of wood and toss it into the water. Moses obeyed and the bitter water immediately became good for drinking! At this time the Lord spoke to His people saying,

> *If thou wilt diligently hearken to the voice of the Lord thy God, and wilt do that which is right in his sight, and wilt give ear to his commandments, and keep all his statutes, I will put none of these diseases upon thee, which I have brought upon the Egyptians: for I am the Lord that healeth thee.*
>
> *Exodus 15:26*

From here, the Israelite's traveled from place to place by the Lord's continued guidance. It was after one month of traveling the Israelites again began complaining to Moses and Aaron, only this time it was about their lack of food. They began voicing grumblings on how they would've been better off dead in Egypt instead of starving in the desert (Ex 16:3). Hearing their complaints, The Lord informed Moses He was going to supply their daily need for bread in a miraculous way! Here is what God did: In the mornings they would find bread which would come down from heaven covering the ground. It was unlike anything ever seen, so they called it, manna, which means "What is it?" [65]Two months after their exodus from Egypt, God brought the Israelites to Mount Sinai and had them camp at its base. If you remember, this is the mountain where God first spoke to Moses in the burning bush. Once again Moses climbed Sinai and the Lord spoke to him saying,

> *Thus shalt thou say to the house of Jacob, and tell the children of Israel; Ye have seen what I did unto the Egyptians, and how I bare you on eagles' wings, and brought you unto myself. Now therefore, if ye will obey my voice indeed, and keep my covenant, then ye shall be a peculiar treasure unto me above all people: for all the earth is mine: And ye shall be unto me a kingdom of priests, and an holy nation. These are the words which thou shalt speak unto the children of Israel.*

> *Exodus 19:3-6*

Returning to the base of the mountain, Moses presented The Lord's message to the people of Israel, and they responded with one voice saying, *"All that the Lord hath spoken we will do" (Ex 19:8)*. Looking back, the covenant God had made with Abraham centered on how a nation would come from his descendants. God's focus was to build a *"kingdom of priests and an holy nation" (Ex 19:6)*. When God spoke to Moses on the mountain there were over two million people who had descended from Abraham, Isaac, and Jacob. As far as population goes, one can easily see God was indeed building His nation from Abraham's seed, a peculiar people led by *His* hand and obeying *His* laws.

God's Law

Soon after the Israelites committed to obey God, He gave them 10 commandments as the basic standard of moral living for His covenant people. The commandments are found in *Exodus* 20:2-17. In a brief summary they are:

1. Do not have other gods before God.
2. Do not make an idolatrous image that you worship.
3. Do not take God's name in vain.
4. Remember to keep the sabbath day holy. (Please reference Appendix II on page 201.)
5. Honor your parents.
6. Do not kill.
7. Do no commit adultery.
8. Do not steal.
9. Do not lie.
10. Do not covet your neighbors possessions.

After God finished pronouncing these 10 commandments, the people fell into great fear (Ex 20:18). Straightaway, the Israelites spoke to Moses saying, *"Speak thou with us, and we will hear: but let not God speak with us, lest we die (Ex 20:19).* Moses obliged the people and soon returned to the top of Mount Sinai for 40 days and nights to hear from the voice of the Lord. During this time, God presented to Moses the 10 commandments written with His own finger on two stone tablets! As well, Moses wrote down additional Israelite laws which God dictated to him. At the end of the 40 days, Moses descended the mountain to find the Israelites severely corrupting themselves in wickedness. They had taken the gold acquired from the Egyptians and cast themselves a golden calf. The Israelites were degenerately worshipping it as a god. As Moses came further down the mountain he was able to behold their wicked actions, and with indignation he smashed the precious commandments he had received from God.

Moses brought order back into the camp and had the golden calf destroyed. He then interceded for the Israelites' lives because the Lord was full of wrath at their actions (Ex 32:31). Still the Lord judged those who had sinned (Ex 32:31). Soon after this Israelite scandal, God called Moses back up the mountain where he remained another 40 days and nights. This time God had Moses chisel out the 10 commandments on the stone tablets. During this encounter on the mountain God instructed Moses by saying, *"Write thou these words: for after the tenor of these words I have made a covenant with thee and with Israel" (Ex 34:27).* The Bible provides evidence that Moses wrote much of the first five books of the Bible during this time (Ex 24:7-8; 34:27-28; Dt 31:9; Jo 1:7-8; 1Kg 2:3).

While on the mountain God instructed Moses to write down 613 laws He was giving to His covenant people to follow.[66] Each commandment had to do with every area of life for the Hebrew people, and as God's chosen nation they were required to follow them. These 613 laws can be grouped into the following categories: moral, religious, ceremonial, social, criminal, dietary, sacrificial, and civil. These laws are found in the books of *Exodus*, *Leviticus*, and *Deuteronomy*. God, in His infinite wisdom, had a purpose for each law given. The Israelites were a people without a human king. They were solely dependent on God for building and governing their entire way of life. When Moses came down from Mount Sinai the second time, the people looked upon him and became fearful, for his face radiated the light of God. Moses then gathered all the children of Israel together and imparted to them *all* of God's Words (Ex 24:3, 7).

Later in his life, Moses reminded the Israelites of God's commandments for His covenant people to live by. After declaring God's Word to the people Moses said,

> *Now these are the commandments, the statutes, and the judgments, which the Lord your God commanded to teach you, that ye might do them in the land whither ye go to possess it: That thou mightest fear the Lord thy God, to keep all his statutes and his commandments, which I command thee, thou, and thy son, and thy son's son, all the days of thy life; and that thy days may be prolonged. Hear therefore, O Israel, and observe to do it; that it may be well with thee, and that ye may increase mightily, as the Lord God of thy fathers hath promised thee, in the land that floweth with milk and honey. Hear,*

*O Israel: The Lord our God is one Lord: And thou shalt
love the Lord thy God with all thine heart, and with all
thy soul, and with all thy might. And these words, which I
command thee this day, shall be in thine heart: And thou
shalt teach them diligently unto thy children, and shalt
talk of them when thou sittest in thine house, and when
thou walkest by the way, and when thou liest down, and
when thou risest up. And thou shalt bind them for a sign
upon thine hand, and they shall be as frontlets between
thine eyes. And thou shalt write them upon the posts of
thy house, and on thy gates.*

Deuteronomy 6:1-9

In this passage Moses not only reminds the Israelites to keep all of
God's commandments, but to also teach them to their children by
talking about them morning, noon, and night!

Israel In The Desert

From Sinai, the Israelites were led by God onward to conquer all the land He had promised to their ancestors. When the Israelites were nearing the land of the Amorites (the first place they
were directed to conquer) they sent 12 men to scout the land. The
scouts soon returned to give a report. 10 of the men came back fear-
fully anxious, sowing their doubts and fears among the Israelites
that they could never be victorious over such strong people. Two of
the scouts however, were not afraid, but confident God would give
them victory. These two brave warriors, Joshua and Caleb, did their
best to stir up courage in the Israelite's faint and faithless hearts, but
to no avail. Fear had taken hold of the people so much they even
desired to stone the two valiant men (Nu 14:10)! The Bible tells us
God was disappointed in His people for their faithlessness. Had He
not delivered them time and time again, and provided for their
needs? Yet they still were unfaithful and doubtful, not trusting in
His provision and protection. Because of the Israelite's rebellious
decision, God chose not to lead them directly into the promised
land, but rather let them wander in the desert 40 years until that

untrusting generation passed away. Joshua and Caleb, however, re-mained alive during this time since God had promised they would enter the promised land because of their faithfulness. Moses had also disappointed the Lord during their travels by incorrectly han-dling God's instruction. Because of this, God would not permit even Moses to enter the promised land (Nu 20:7-12). The Lord allowed Moses to live and lead the people through the desert during their 40 year punishment, but at the close of this period, at the age of 120 years, God took Moses home into eternity (Dt 34:7). Up until the time of Moses' death, the Scriptures tell us his eyes and body were still strong! Moses had ushered God's chosen people to the doorstep of the promised land, the Jordan river. God then appointed Joshua to be the next leader of His people, the one to help Israel claim the land of God's promise. Throughout their 40-year wanderings in the desert, **the Lord bestowed His people with continuous miracles for the purpose of showing them again and again He is the One and only true God, the Creator of the heavens and earth (Nm 13-14; Dt 1).**

Joshua

The next man to lead God's chosen people was Joshua, son of Nun. If you remember, he was one of the 12 scouts Moses had sent to survey the promised land shortly after the Israelites had re-ceived God's laws on the Mountain of Sinai. 10 of the 12 scouts spread fear to the people through their lack of faith in God's mighty hand. Due to their disobedience, God postponed their covenantal inheritance by 40 years of wandering in the desert. Joshua and Caleb were the only ones who trusted God. Because of their courage and faithfulness to the Lord, God blessed them with added years so they were able to enter the promised land and did not die off with the faithless generation in the desert. The Bible says Joshua was full of the spirit of wisdom and the Israelites were obedient to Joshua, as they were to Moses (Dt 34:9). When Moses passed away, the Lord

told Joshua to lead the Israelites to take possession of the promised
land:

> *From the wilderness and this Lebanon even unto the
> great river, the river Euphrates, all the land of the Hit-
> tites, and unto the great sea toward the going down of the
> sun, shall be your coast. There shall not any man be able
> to stand before thee all the days of thy life: as I was with
> Moses, so I will be with thee: I will not fail thee, nor for-
> sake thee.*

Joshua 1:4-5

For the first time God was informing His people what the border
lines of the promised land were. Wandering in the desert those
many years, Joshua probably became familiar with the surrounding
geography of this land. Once God commissioned the new leader of
Israel, He encouraged him by saying,

> *Be strong and of a good courage: for unto this people
> shalt thou divide for an inheritance the land, which I
> sware [swore] unto their fathers to give them. Only be
> thou strong and very courageous, that thou mayest ob-
> serve to do according to all the law, which Moses my
> servant commanded thee: turn not from it to the right
> hand or to the left, that thou mayest prosper withersoever
> thou goest. This book of the law shall not depart out of
> thy mouth; but thou shalt meditate therein day and night,
> that thou mayest observe to do according to all that is
> written therein: for then thou shalt make thy way pros-
> perous, and then thou shalt have good success. Have not
> I commanded thee? Be strong and of a good courage; be
> not afraid, neither be thou dismayed: for the Lord thy
> God is with thee whithersoever thou goest.*

Joshua 1:6-9

Although the Bible does not reveal Joshua's words to the Lord at
this time, the Scriptures do tell us the actions he took. Immediately,
Joshua had his officers inform all the people to prepare provisions
and make ready! The report went out to the people, *"within three
days ye shall pass over this Jordan, to go in to possess the land, which the*

Lord your God giveth you to possess it" (Jo 1:11). Jericho was the first
city west of the Jordan they were to conquer. Before the Israelites
made their move, Joshua sent in two scouts to spy out the land. The
scouts returned and reported, *"Truly the Lord hath delivered into our
hands all the land; for even all the inhabitants of the country do faint because of us" (Jo 2:24).* Joshua 3 records yet another miracle God performed for His people; He stopped the flowing of the Jordan river so
the people could walk across on dry ground! It seems that one of
God's purposes in this miracle was to show He was with Joshua as
He was with Moses. Once the people had all crossed the river,
Joshua set up 12 stones representing the 12 tribes of Israel as a reminder of God's miraculous provision. Joshua told the people to
explain to their children these stones are a reminder that:

> *Israel came over this Jordan on dry land. For the Lord
> your God dried up the waters of Jordan from before you,
> until ye were passed over, as the Lord your God did to
> the Red sea, which he dried up from before us, until we
> were gone over: That all the people of the earth might
> know the hand of the Lord, that it is mighty: that ye
> might fear the Lord your God for ever.*

> *Joshua 4:22-24*

The time was approaching to march onward, but before
Joshua led the people to conquer Jericho, he first circumcised all the
men born in the desert during the 40-years of wandering. Remember, circumcision was the sign of God's covenant with Abraham. Circumcision showed they indeed belonged to the covenantal blessings
of the Lord. While the men were recovering from their surgery, the
Israelites celebrated the Passover meal, commemorating God's protection during the 10th plague of Egypt. On the following day, the
people gathered some local produce for themselves. Starting that
day, the manna God had miraculously supplied for His people
stopped appearing and was never seen again (Jo 5:12). God seemed

to be showing His people He was going to provide for them through the abundance of the fruitful promised land from here on out!

The day had come for the Israelites to take possession of the land God had given them. Jericho was the first city of many to be conquered (Jo 6:2). The book of *Joshua* records how the Israelites took the land town by town which God had promised to Abraham, Isaac, and Jacob. All throughout his years of leadership, Joshua guided the people by the grace of God. By the time Joshua was an old man, God had blessed His people with victory over the majority of their covenantal promised land. After three years of peace in their new land, a very old Joshua called all the leadership of his people together and said:

> *...ye have seen all that the Lord your God hath done unto all these nations because of you; for the Lord your God is he that hath fought for you. Behold, I have divided unto you by lot these nations that remain, to be an inheritance for your tribes, from Jordan, with all the nations that I have cut off, even unto the great sea westward. And the Lord your God, he shall expel them from before you, and drive them from out of your sight; and ye shall possess their land, as the Lord your God hath promised unto you. Be ye therefore very courageous to keep and to do all that is written in the book of the law of Moses, that ye turn not aside therefrom to the right hand or to the left; That ye come not among these nations, these that remain among you; neither make mention of the name of their gods, nor cause to swear by them, neither serve them, nor bow yourselves unto them: But cleave unto the Lord your God, as ye have done unto this day. For the Lord hath driven out from before you great nations and strong: but as for you, no man hath been able to stand before you unto this day. One man of you shall chase a thousand: for the Lord your God, he it is that fighteth for you, as he hath promised you. Take good heed therefore unto yourselves, that ye love the Lord your God.*

> *Joshua 23:2-11*

Joshua is reminding his people it was God who wiped out their enemies and gifted them with the promised land. He encouraged them to remain faithful to God's laws, and take heed to never follow the false gods of the people whose land they now controlled.

Sometimes people wonder why God wiped out those nations, thinking it is wrong and unjust. What they fail to see is that these people hated God and chose to live wickedly before Him. These nations were living contrary to God's Words. Their forefathers had run from Babel after the language mix-up and continued doing evil in the sight of the Lord. They filled the land with idolatry and other atrocious sins (Ex 34:11-16; Dt 7:1-5; 20:16-18). Their consistent rebellion grieved their Creator. They had rejected Him with their thoughts, actions, and hearts. So, He judged them, just as He had done with Adam and Eve, and just as He will do with you and me. God created everything and everyone. He knows our every thought, intent, and action. **The Lord alone has the wisdom to execute perfect justice.** Since the people on earth had rejected Him yet again, God had a plan that began with Abraham to raise up a people who would joyfully obey their Maker. The Israelites and their leaders were not perfect, but God chose to reveal Himself to them and give them His standard for living in the laws presented to Moses on Mount Sinai. In *Leviticus* 20:24 God said to Moses, *"Ye shall inherit their land, and I will give it unto you to possess it, a land that floweth with milk and honey: I am the Lord your God, which have separated you from other people."* God created Israel to be different in a world which had rebelled against Him. He carefully formed this nation slowly over time, refining their character through trials along the way. **When the time was right, He gave them their land of promise, and at the same time used them to cleanse it from the darkness of sin those inhabiting it had come to idolize.** Israel had been commanded by God to *fully* wipe out the people of the land. God had them do this so the sins of these people groups would not seep into the lives of His chosen people and corrupt them (Ex 34:11-16; Nu 33:51-56; Dt 20:16-18).

God had a divine purpose for the nation of Israel. What was that purpose? The Lord told Moses Israel was to be *"a kingdom of priests, and an holy nation" (Ex 19:5-6)*. God's purpose in forming Israel involved them being the light of truth to all the people of the world. In Joshua's old age he reminds the Hebrews who they were created to be; A separate, holy nation formed by the hand of God. He reminds them of these truths so they do not fall into the trap of becoming prideful by rejecting the Lord and experiencing God's judgement themselves.

At the end of Joshua's life he gave one final address. The speech is an overview of what God had done beginning with Abraham up to their present time. He explained human power did not get them where they were. No, God was their Provider. In closing his address Joshua spoke these words to the Israelite people saying:

> *...fear the Lord, and serve him in sincerity and in truth: and put away the gods which your fathers served on the other side of the flood, and in Egypt; and serve ye the Lord. And if it seem evil unto you to serve the Lord, choose you this day whom ye will serve; whether the gods which your fathers served that were on the other side of the flood, or the gods of the Amorites, in whose land ye dwell: but as for me and my house, we will serve the Lord.*

> *Joshua 24:14-15*

Joshua encouraged the Israelites to choose whether they would serve the One true God, or the invented gods of the people whose land they had conquered. Adamantly, the people agreed they would serve the Lord (Jo 24:21-22, 24). God's promise to Abraham, regarding the promised land, had been fulfilled during Joshua's leadership! Joshua passed away at the age of 110, joining his forefathers in God's Kingdom.

From this day forward, it was up to the Israelites to choose to be a kingdom of priests, for God always gives us a free will to choose (Ex 19:6). God had raised them up to be a beacon of light, representing His truth to the whole world. There was, however, one major problem: the Israelites often chose to live in sin.They possessed God's law, but the law does not save anyone. The purpose of God's law is to show us how high God's standard is for righteousness, and that there is no way one could live up to it perfectly. This truth is also part of God's plan and storyline for the Israelites and us. **The Lord does not leave us without a remedy to overcome sin and its consequences.** But this hope is revealed later in the climax of God's story.

Throughout Joshua's life and the lives of the elders who outlived Joshua, Israel served the Lord (Jo 24:31). Not long after Joshua's leadership ended, the Israelites took possession of the remaining land, but they did not *fully* destroy the wicked as God had commanded (Dt 20:16-18). Because of their disobedience, all too soon a generation rose up in Israel who did not know the Lord or what mighty things He had done for their forefathers (Jd 2:10-13).

Judges
The book of *Judges*, the seventh book in the Bible, follows chronologically after the reign of Joshua. God begins this book by detailing the Israelite's continued pursuit of claiming the remaining parts of the land God had promised to Abraham (Jd 1). Regrettably, the Israelites failed to entirely wipe out the people dwelling in the land. **The people's false gods and wicked teachings quickly corrupted the Israelites (Dt 20:16-18).**

In *Judges* 2 the Lord spoke to the Israelite people about their disobedience through an angel saying,

> *I made you to go up out of Egypt, and have brought you unto the land which I sware [swore] unto your fathers; and I said, I will never break my covenant with you. And ye shall make no league with the inhabitants of this land; ye shall throw down their altars: but ye have not obeyed my voice: why have ye done this? Wherefore I also said, I will not drive them out from before you; but they shall be as thorns in your sides, and their gods shall be a snare unto you. And it came to pass, when the angel of the Lord spake [spoke] these words unto all the children of Israel, that the people lifted up their voice, and wept.*

Judges 2:1-4

In this passage God is reminding His people the covenant He had made with them required their obedience in not making allegiances with their enemies. They failed, however, to obey Him. Therefore, the Lord decreed that their enemies were to remain in the land, *"as thorns in their sides."* **The Scriptures record how the people wept at God's message, but one wonders if their weeping ever turned to repenting.**

As was mentioned earlier, the people who occupied the promised land were wicked. God instructed the Israelites to completely wipe them out because if God's people did not their enemies would pollute the Israelites with their sinful ways. Eventually, their enemies worship of false god's would influence them, infecting their nation with a disease of lies against the truth of God's Word. As time went on, God's warnings and cautions were abandoned and the infection of sin spread into the Israelite's lives, poisoning them toward God and His ways. They willingly chose to worship their neighbor's strange and false gods. When the Israelites chose rebellion after ample and continual warnings, God gave His people over to their enemies and ceased to defend them in battle. Yet the Lord's eyes were still on His people, and He had compassion on them when they cried out to Him with sincere and repentant hearts. God's merciful hand is proved mighty for those who turn from their sins and follow after Him.

At the time appointed, God answered the cries of the Israelites for deliverance. He raised up for them a judge who would lead them back to Himself and liberate them from oppression. These judges God raised up had a more prominent role than local leaders; they were often military warriors "empowered by God's Holy Spirit for the deliverance and preservation of Israel..."[67] Once the people had been rescued by a judge, Israel would have peace and would serve the Lord... until the judge's death. When a judge died, the people foolishly sunk back into their wicked habits and behaviors, abandoning the true God of Israel for the worship of false gods and idols made in the imaginations of men (Jd 2). Just as God did in the past, He allowed the ungodly nations to live in the land for the purpose of proving Israel's faithful obedience to Him.

The first judge God raised up for the Israelites was Othniel. At that time, the Israelites had been under the oppression of the king of Mesopatamia for eight years. Being weary of their suppression, the Israelites cried out the the Lord. Hearing their plea for redemption God raised up Othniel, who was Caleb's younger brother. (If you remember, Caleb was one of the 12 spies whom Moses sent out. He and Joshua were the only two who returned in courage while the other 10 were afraid and faithless.) The Bible says,

> ...the Spirit of the Lord came upon him [Othniel], and he judged Israel, and went out to war: and the Lord delivered Chushanrishathaim king of Mesopotamia into his hand; and his hand prevailed against Chushanrishathaim.

> *Judges 3:10*

This judge brought peace to Israel for 40 years, but after his death the people rejected The Lord, doing evil in His sight. God then allowed Israel to again be overtaken and oppressed for 18 more years. Just as before, the people cried out to the Lord because of their hardship so He raised up the second judge, Ehud. Ehud judged for 80 years, rescuing the Israelites and bringing peace to the land.

Throughout the book of *Judges* the Israelites repeatedly reject God, He delivers them into the hands of their enemies, God's people cry out to Him, He raises up a judge to deliver them, the judge rescues them from their enemies, and there is peace in the land... until the judge dies. Mournfully, the people once again would follow after false god's, and the whole pitiful cycle continued over and over again.

Judges provides interesting stories which give us great insight into Israel's struggles and victories in their relationship with God. As we watch God's story unfold, we may ask the question, Has God written a story in which people have a free will, or has He written a horrific story where He dictates the destinies of every person? The answer to this question is: **People *do* have a free will to make decisions, while God is intimately involved in the daily workings of men.** Let's think back to when God made Adam and Eve. He gave them a free will to choose whether or not they would eat from the tree. Their decision was made, and the earth has suffered the consequences of their choice, as we still do today. Yet, God foreknew they were going to make the decision they made. Likewise, God knew the Israelites would reject Him continually before He promised Abraham a great nation would come from his seed. **The Lord did not choose to create the nation of Israel because they were more special than the rest of the people on the planet, but simply because He was keeping His oath with Abraham, and had a greater plan in mind!** God owns the pen to His storyline! Though He owns the pen, He gives people the free will to make decisions. Since God is outside of time, unlike us, He already knows the choices every person will make before they are born. Therefore, **when God intervenes in the lives of men He does so with the foreknowledge of what the person's course of action would be if He never intervened.** People have a free will to choose to obey the Lord or reject Him: this includes every person on the planet, not just the people of Israel. Likewise, God is the Author and has the free will to write His script, foreknowing everyone's decisions ahead of time, with every word He writes, like an unbeatable master chess player!

Despite the Israelite's numerous rejections of the Lord, God is faithful to them because He loves His people (Dt 7:8). God's plan was for them to be a kingdom of priests and a holy nation on the earth, representing Him. Sadly, the Israelites didn't obey the Lord with all their heart as they'd professed they would. Yet, again we have to remember God owns the pen and knew the Israelites would reject Him. God's plan was bigger than just creating a holy nation! **When God spoke to Abraham, telling him the whole earth would be blessed through his seed, the Lord was making an extraordinary promise on a deeper level than just to the nation of Israel.** Thus far we see clearly the nation of Israel was struggling with being a holy nation. So, what could God be referring to? Did His plan fail? Absolutely not! As we proceed onward we watch as more of God's divine storyline continues through the prophets He sends to His people, and the kings He allows to rule over them!

Prophets & Kings

In the Bible a prophet was someone whom God chose to reveal His messages through. Noah was a prophet. God spoke to him about His coming judgement, and Noah warned the people. As well,

Abraham, Isaac, and Jacob were prophets. God spoke to them, too. Although there were prophets before the nation of Israel was born, the term *prophet* in the Bible most often refers to a few select Israelites. God used these prophets to broadcast His messages to individuals and nations, especially the nation of Israel. In fact, the Israelites were the ones who had pleaded with Moses for God to speak to them through a prophet. If you remember, Israel was in great dread upon hearing the voice of the Lord declaring the 10 commandments. They drew back in fear and asked the Lord to communicate through Moses. God obliged them, and since that day He continued to speak to His people through a prophet.

The word *prophet* is found in the KJV Bible 491 times in 455 verses. Some of these verses refer to false prophets, that is, people who claim to speak for God but are liars, or people who claim to speak for false gods. When God spoke to Moses on Mount Sinai He gave him a clear way to distinguish between true and false prophets. The Lord said, *"When a prophet speaketh in the name of the Lord, if the thing follow not, nor come to pass, that is the thing which the Lord hath not spoken, but the prophet hath spoken it presumptuously: thou shalt not be afraid of him" (Dt 18:22).* In other words, if a "prophet" speaks in God's name and his words do not come true, then they are a liar. Furthermore, God gave one more directive about prophets. In *Deuteronomy* 13 God informed Moses that if a prophet's words come true and that "prophet" leads you to worship false gods then do not listen to him. Throughout the Israelite's history prophets played a big role in communicating God's message, not only for their present time, but also for the future. God used the words of a prophet or what is called "prophecy" to proclaim judgement, blessing, or a future event.

The first traditional prophet mentioned in the Scriptures is a man named Samuel. There are two books of the Bible, *1* and *2*

Samuel, named after this prophet. The Lord used Samuel to speak to His people. *"...All Israel from Dan even to Beersheba knew that Samuel was established to be a prophet of the Lord. ...And the word of Samuel came to all Israel" (1 Sa 3:20; 4:1).* Not only was Samuel a prophet, but he also served as the last judge of Israel. In *1 Samuel* 7 we read how he led the Israelites to victory over their enemies, the Philistines, by God's gracious hand. However, when Samuel grew old the Israelites expressed how they longed for a king to rule over them, like their neighboring nations. Samuel was appalled at their request. The nation of Israel had never had a ruler over them! All their laws were given to them by God. God was Israel's King. Nevertheless, the Bible says Samuel laid their request before the Lord. God responded by saying,

> *...hearken unto the voice of the people in all that they say unto thee: for they have not rejected thee, but they have rejected me, that I should not reign over them. According to all the works which they have done since the day that I brought them up out of Egypt even unto this day, wherewith they have forsaken me, and served other gods, so do they also unto thee. Now therefore hearken unto their voice: howbeit yet protest solemnly unto them, and shew [show] them the manner of the king that shall reign over them.*

> *1 Samuel 8:7-9*

Samuel obeyed the Lord. He warned the people about the power a king would have over the nation. He warned them, but they were persistent. They shook off Samuel's counsel and said *"...we will have a king over us; That we also may be like all the nations; and that our king may judge us, and go out before us, and fight our battles" (1 Sa 8:19-20).*

God chose for the Israelites their first king and revealed whom it would be to His prophet, Samuel. Having gathered all of Israel together, Samuel made the grand announcement, revealing their new ruler's identity. As soon as the people heard the news they shouted with excitement saying *"...God save the king" (1 Sa 10:24)*. When the people's cheers subsided, Samuel explained how Israel's new kingdom government would function *"...and wrote it in a book, and laid it up before the Lord. And Samuel sent all the people away, every man to his house" (1 Sa 10:25)*. Sometime later Samuel spoke again to all the people of Israel, reminding them that their request for a king had been granted, nevertheless, they were always to keep in mind God was still their great King.

> *If ye will fear the Lord, and serve him, and obey his voice, and not rebel against the commandment of the Lord, then shall both ye and also the king that reigneth over you continue following the Lord your God: But if ye will not obey the voice of the Lord, but rebel against the commandment of the Lord, then shall the hand of the Lord be against you, as it was against your fathers. Now therefore stand and see this great thing, which the Lord will do before your eyes. Is it not wheat harvest to day? I will call unto the Lord, and he shall send thunder and rain; that ye may perceive and see that your wickedness is great, which ye have done in the sight of the Lord, in asking you a king. So Samuel called unto the Lord; and the Lord sent thunder and rain that day: and all the people greatly feared the Lord and Samuel. And all the people said unto Samuel, Pray for thy servants unto the Lord thy God, that we die not: for we have added unto all our sins this evil, to ask us a king. And Samuel said unto the people, Fear not: ye have done all this wickedness: yet turn not aside from following the Lord, but serve the Lord with all your heart; And turn ye not aside: for then should ye go after vain things, which cannot profit nor deliver; for they are vain. For the Lord will not forsake his people for his great name's sake: because it hath pleased the Lord to make you his people. Moreover as for me, God forbid that I should sin against the Lord in ceasing to pray for you: but I will teach you the good and the right way: Only fear the Lord, and serve him in truth with all your heart: for consider how great things he hath done for you. But if ye shall still do wickedly, ye shall be consumed, both ye and your king.*

> *1 Samuel 12:14-25*

Samuel's prayer and God's response with thunder and rain was additional proof Samuel was a true prophet of the Lord. Samuel warned them about the consequences of a kingdom government but the people refused to listen. Sadly, Scripture records the majority of Israel's kings were wicked. However, there were a a few righteous kings God rose up who turned the people's hearts back to Himself, just like the earlier judges had. All of the kings of Israel were significant, but for our overview purpose we will look briefly at the reigns of the first three kings: Saul, David, and Solomon.

Saul

Saul was the first king of Israel God directed Samuel to anoint. Mournfully, at the very start of Saul's reign he willfully disobeyed one of the commands given to him by the Lord. The Lord was displeased and sent Samuel the prophet to speak to him saying, *"...thy kingdom shall not continue: the Lord hath sought him a man after his own heart, and the Lord hath commanded him to be captain over his people, because thou hast not kept that which the Lord commanded thee..."* *(1 Sa 13:13)*. Although these words were declared to Saul at the beginning of his reign, they were actually prophetic in meaning, speaking of future events. God allowed Saul to continue ruling as king for a time, for **even amidst Saul's rebellious actions, God used him to further unfold His divine storyline!** One way God used him was by sending him into war against Israel's enemies, the Amalekites. The Lord spoke to Saul through the prophet Samuel saying,

> *...I remember that which Amalek did to Israel, how he laid wait for him in the way, when he came up from Egypt. Now go and smite Amalek, and utterly destroy all that they have, and spare them not; but slay both man and woman, infant and suckling, ox and sheep, camel and ass [donkey].*

> *1 Samuel 15:2-3*

Saul and his army defeated the Amalekites, but in his rebellion, Saul did not fully obey what the Lord instructed. The Bible says Saul *"...spared Agag [king of Amalek], and the best of the sheep, and of the oxen, and of the fatlings, and the lambs, and all that was good, and would not utterly destroy them..." (1 Sa 15:9).* The Lord was greatly displeased at His anointed king's actions, and immediately sent His prophet, Samuel, to confront Saul (1 Sa 15:10). Pridefully, Saul justified his actions, but Samuel spoke words from the Lord saying, *"rebellion is as the sin of witchcraft, and stubbornness is as iniquity and idolatry. Because thou hast rejected the word of the Lord, he hath also rejected thee from being king" (1 Sa 15:23).* After Samuel delivered God's message, Saul finally confessed his sin. That fateful day finally came to an end, and Samuel never met face to face with Saul again, nevertheless Samuel mourned for Saul. God spoke to Samuel telling him to mourn no longer for even now He had chosen another to be the next king of Israel. This next king would be the one who would follow after the Lord's heart and whom would seek to honor The Lord in his life (1 Kg 2:2). This king to be was David, son of Jesse.

David

Not long after Samuel and Saul's last meeting, God led Samuel to the little town of Bethlehem. It was here he was to anoint one of Jesse's eight sons the next king of Israel. Unexpectedly, The Lord directed Samuel to anoint the youngest boy, David. The Bible says as soon as David was anointed God's Spirit came upon him. The next verse tells us God's Spirit left King Saul, and an evil spirit came and troubled him. Although the young David had been anointed to be king, God did not present him the throne right away. The Lord spent the next 10-20 years teaching David godly character and wisdom before he began to reign (1 Sa 16:11-13; 2 Sa 5:4). Interestingly, part of David's education involved working in King Saul's court as a musician. When an evil spirit came upon Saul, the only thing found to soothe his anger was the sounds of harp music. As only the greatest Author would have it, God had, for this very occasion, gifted David with the skill and talent to play the harp beautifully. Saul's servants knew of David's musical gifting and sent for him. Upon hearing the sweet-sounding music from David's accomplished hands, King Saul's anger was pacified (1 Sa 16).

David played the harp for King Saul from time to time when the king needed a peaceful song to calm his anger. During this period of time, David would travel back and forth from his home, where he took care of his family's flock. One day David's father, Jesse, instructed him to take some extra provisions to his elder brothers who were in the Israelite army. As David approached the Israelite camp, he saw there was a standoff between the Israelite's and their enemies, the Philistines. To his surprise, there was a giant over nine feet tall taunting the Israelites and blaspheming God's name (1 Sa 17:4; 8-10). When David heard his words he said, *"...who is this uncircumcised Philistine that he should defy the armies of the living God" (1 Sa 17:26)?* David's eldest brother overheard these words and angrily scolded David, accusing him of coming down just to watch the battle. David's bold saying was told to King Saul. David then went to Saul and assured him he would fight this giant, Goliath. Saul doubted David's military ability, after all, he was just a youth! Despite his age, David was confident the Lord would rescue him from the giant Philistine. **Strapping on his armor of faith, and only his sling in his hand, the young warrior stepped onto the battlefield!** David and Goliath approached one another on the grassy plain and exchanged words. Goliath scoffed at David's choice of weapon. David replied by saying,

> *Thou comest to me with a sword, and with a spear, and with a shield: but I come to thee in the name of the Lord of hosts, the God of the armies of Israel, whom thou hast defied. This day will the Lord deliver thee into mine hand; and I will smite thee, and take thine head from thee; and I will give the carcases of the host of the Philis-*

tines this day unto the fowls of the air, and to the wild
beasts of the earth; that all the earth may know that there
is a God in Israel. And all this assembly shall know that
the Lord saveth not with sword and spear: for the battle
is the Lord's, and he will give you into our hands.

1 Samuel 17:45-47

At this, Goliath moved in to fight David and David ran toward the giant, launching a stone from his sling directly at the head of the blasphemous Philistine. The stone hit its mark, sinking into Goliath's forehead, which caused him to slump to the ground, dead. Immediately, David ran toward the Philistine and cut off his head with Goliath's own sword. This victory for the Israelites brought joy to Saul and his army, but terror throughout the Philistine camp. The Philistines ran for their lives with the Israelites pursuing hot on their heels.

King Saul was greatly impressed with David's victory. So much so he would not allow him to return home, but hired him to work full time in his governmental cabinet. David remained with Saul, bringing him great victory again and again. David was so successful Saul made him a commander over the army of Israel (1 Sa 18:5). As David became more and more triumphant over their enemies, the people began to sing his praises, and jealousy stirred in Saul's heart. Traveling through different towns, Saul overheard songs boasting of David's great victories saying, *"Saul hath slain his thousands, and David his ten thousands" (1 Sa 18:7).* This song enraged Saul's jealous feelings toward David. His envious feelings grew and grew, and one day Saul chucked his spear at David, but failed to kill him. David escaped with his life by the grace of God. After his attempt to take David's life, Saul feared David. The king knew the young warrior had The Lord's favor and also the hearts of the people. Saul hoped to rid himself of David by giving him command over 1,000 men and sending him off into thick battle. But David did not die, he continued being victorious in battle after battle. Saul's frustrated jealousy only mounted and he asked his servants to murder his former harpist (1 Sa 19:1). Saul's son, Jonathan, had become David's closest and devoted friend. Aware of his father's plan to execute David, Jonathan warned him of the evil plans against his life. David took heed and fled into the mountains, living away from his home for many years. During that time he gathered with him a band of 600 men who were in some kind of misfortune. Together they fought their enemies, and kept one step ahead of Saul's hot pursuing army. Hoping to take David's life and soothe his jealous rage, Saul relentlessly continued to track David and his band of loyal men. Saul's many designs to end David's life never succeeded, but ironically it was King Saul who was eventually slaughtered in battle against an enemy army. Once Saul was killed, the Kingdom of Israel needed a new king to lead their nation (1 Sa 22 - 31).

David was a young lad tending his father's sheep when he'd been anointed to be king of Israel. He had patiently waited on God's timing to give him the throne, and during the passing years had become a skilled warrior and leader. God had prepared him and was now ready to give him the ruling throne. After Saul had been slain the kingdom split. The tribe of Judah recognized David as king and remained loyal to him, but the commander of Saul's army, Abner, acted quickly, proclaiming Saul's son, Ishbosheth, king of all the other tribes of Israel. Seven and a half years later the political winds blew, bringing all the tribes of Israel under the command of David's crown (2 Sa 2-5). Throughout David's Kingship he had great military victory.

Of all the King's of Israel, more is written about David's life than any other. There are many lessons one can learn from the life of David. David's heart desired mightily to please the Lord, and God even encouraged future kings to follow in King David's commitments to The Lord (1 Kg 9:4; 15:3-5). David was not always wise however, and at times gave way to temptation and severely transgressed God's law, grieving His Creator. **God judged and punished David for his acts of sin, but also had compassion on him because of David's sincere repentance.** Despite David's failures God was greatly pleased with him, so much so that God made a covenant with him and his descendants: The covenant was that David would have a family member to rule from the throne of Israel forever (2 Sa 7:5-29; Ps 89:3-4). (Please reference Appendix I on page 198 to learn more about covenants.) **In David's youth he was a shepherd watching over his father's flock. In his adult life David was a shepherd watching over his Heavenly Father's flock, the people of Israel.** David was a great king, arguably the greatest earthly king Israel ever had. David was a man who loved to play music, sing songs, and write down the words in his heart. He penned most of the *Psalms*, which is a book in the Bible containing 150 different songs written to the Lord. This is an amazing book recording just about every experience and emotion one may go through in this life.

As David neared the end of his journey on earth his son, Adonijah, gathered a great crowd and announced himself as the new king of all Israel. The people hearing the news gave a rousing cheer. David was still on the throne however, and had not pronounced this son his successor. When David heard what Adonijah had done, he took swift action and announced to the kingdom that his son, Solomon, was the new king of Israel, crushing Adonijah's plans. David gave Solomon final directions as his life was fading. These councils and commands are found in the second chapter of *1 Kings*, the eleventh book in the Bible. Upon King David's death, Solomon took his rightful position as king and took control of Israel, God's chosen people.

Solomon

Solomon, Israel's third king, inherited the kingdom his father had fought hard and shed blood to establish. David was a king in wartime. Solomon was a king in peacetime. The new king spent his life building Israel up with renowned construction projects, which included the first temple, often referred to as Solomon's Temple.

At the beginning of Solomon's reign the Lord spoke to him in a dream. God asked the young man, *"Ask what shall I give thee" (1 Kg 3:5)?* Solomon did not ask for riches or fame, he answered by saying,

> *O Lord my God, thou hast made thy servant king instead of David my father: and I am but a little child: I know not how to go out or come in. And thy servant is in the midst of thy people which thou hast chosen, a great people, that cannot be numbered nor counted for multitude. Give therefore thy servant an understanding heart to judge thy people, that I may discern between good and bad: for who is able to judge this thy so great a people?*

1 Kings 3:7-9

King Solomon began his reign asking God to bless him with wisdom. Wisdom is what he desired, nothing more. The king's answer pleased God so much He not only blessed him with surpassing wisdom, but with riches and fame because he had not selfishly asked for them. The Kingdom of Israel grew exceedingly prosperous during Solomon's reign. Using the wisdom God bestowed upon him Solomon wrote 3,000 proverbs and 1,005 songs. The book of *Proverbs*, the 20th book of the Bible, was authored by this king of Israel, and of course is inspired by God like every book of the Bible (2 Tm 3:16). *Proverbs* records short sayings of wisdom. Not only was Solomon a writer, but God also gave him an in-depth knowledge about plants and animals of all kinds. The Bible states that distant foreign kingdom's even sent ambassadors to learn from his exceptional wisdom (1 Kg 4).

God also used Solomon to build the first temple, where the Ark of the Covenant was placed, in which the original 10 commandments resided. King David had intended to build this temple, but God would not allow him to because he had shed much blood in wartime. God employed Solomon to complete what his father had in his heart to do and build a consecrated place of worship to the Lord. Solomon began construction on the temple in the fourth year of his reign, which was 480 years after God unshackled his children from the dark bonds of slavery in Egypt. For this building project the king hired 360,000 workers and 3,600 foremen. The temple took seven years to complete. Solomon also built his personal living quarters, a court house, and lastly the king built living quarters for one of his wives, the daughter of Pharaoh (1 Kg 6:38; 7:1-8).

Even though Solomon was the wisest man to have ever lived, he was not perfect. He sinned in one area which brought the downfall of his faithfulness to God. Solomon had a crippling weakness for women. He married many women. In fact, he married 700 women who were of royal blood and also had 300 concubines. Solomon took unto himself 1,000 women! Biblically, marriage is stipulated between one man and one woman. When God brought Adam and Eve together in marriage the Lord stated they were now *"one flesh" (Gn 2:24)*. The act of polygamy destroys God's intentions for a God-honoring, healthy marriage. The Lord warned His covenant people about breaking His instructions in the laws of Moses when He said, *"Neither shall he [the king] multiply wives to himself, that his heart turn not away" (Dt 17:17)*. During this time in history, polygamy was a common transgression and sadly Solomon gave into his wicked lusts.

Furthermore, God had warned the Israelites not to marry foreign women because they would turn their hearts to worship false gods. As forewarned, Solomon's pagan brides did just that. His wives' idolatrous practices drew the wise and honorable king away from the One True God and into the darkness of worshipping false images and the imaginations of men. The Scripture does not clearly tell us whether or not Solomon repented of this sin. Because of Solomon's rebellious heart against God, the Lord spoke the following words to him:

> ...thou hast not kept my covenant and my statutes, which I have commanded thee, I will surely rend the kingdom from thee, and will give it to thy servant. Notwithstanding in thy days I will not do it for David thy father's sake: but I will rend it out of the hand of thy son. Howbeit I will not rend away all the kingdom; but will give one tribe to thy son for David my servant's sake, and for Jerusalem's sake which I have chosen.

1 Kings 11:11-14

Solomon's sin caused the nation of Israel to never be the same. After Solomon's death, the Lord proved faithful to His words. The Kingdom of Israel was split in two with Solomon's son, Rehoboam, ruling as king over the tribes of Judah and Benjamin, and Jeroboam ruling over the other 10 tribes of Israel (1 Kg 12). In the centuries to follow, both of these kingdoms had mostly wicked leadership. Yet, here and there God raised up righteous kings, but even they were compared to the faithfulness of Israel's second king, David.

The kings of Israel and Judah came and went, and the Lord continued to speak through His prophets. One prophet He raised up was a man named Elijah. God used Elijah to display His power and remind His people He alone was the Creator of all, not those powerless, made-up, false gods who many were bowing their knee to (1 Kg 18). God also raised up other prophets while Israel was governed by kings. He sent unto them Isaiah, Jeremiah, Hosea, and others to warn His people about the coming judgements their sin would produce. As more time passed, He raised up Daniel to be a prophet in a foreign land, and to him The Lord unveiled much about the end times. The last prophet recorded in the Old Testament whom God raised up was a man named Malachi. Malachi was given a tremendous message from the Lord to deliver to His people. This prophetic message was that a man was to be born, a man who would announce the coming of the Messiah (Ma 4:5)! **God used each prophet as a trumpet of truth in their own generation.** Many of the messages He gave them were for their present time, but He often spoke to His prophets about the future as well. One such divine prophecy was about a coming King of Israel who would save them once and for all from their enemies (2 Sa 7:11-12; Dn 2:44; 7:14, 27; Is 7:14; 9:6-7; 16:5; Je 23:5; Ob 1:21; Mi 4:7)! The children of Israel waited in great anticipation for this King to make His triumphant appearance and save His people forever!

Over a period of 125 years (722 - 597 B.C.) both Israel and Judah were defeated by foreign militaries and they lost power of their own kingdom, just as the prophets warned.[68] At first it was the Assyrians, then the Babylonians and later the Romans (1 Ch 5:26; 1 Kg 17:5-6; 2 Kg 24:10-16; 25:1-12; Jn 11:48; Ac 22:27-29). The once great nation of Israel became a proxy power, that is, a nation governed by a "puppet" representative appointed by the conquering nation (2 Kg 25:22).

Centuries earlier God had spoken to Abraham the following words:

Get thee out of thy country, and from thy kindred, and from thy father's house, unto a land that I will shew [show] thee: And I will make of thee a great nation, and I will bless thee, and make thy name great; and thou shalt

> *be a blessing: And I will bless them that bless thee, and*
> *curse him that curseth thee: and in thee shall all families*
> *of the earth be blessed.*

Genesis 12:1-3

The Lord proved His words to be true by creating the nation of Israel. Yet, the last part of verse three needs a closer look. God said, *"...in thee shall all families of the earth be blessed."* Was the whole earth blessed through Israel? The nation of Israel had the distinction of power and prestige during the reigns of King David and Solomon, but surely that is not what God was referring to in His prophetic words to Abraham. God had a greater purpose when He created Israel. On one hand God was speaking about Israel. On the other, *more important hand,* God's Words to Abraham alluded to the distant future. He was speaking about how the whole earth would be blessed when the Creator God Himself, descended through Israel! **The God of Abraham, Isaac, and Jacob would put on flesh and walk onto the scene of His script!** The next chapter will reveal the full purpose and meaning of God's words to Abraham through the earthly life of the God-Man, Jesus Christ!

Chapter Four

JESUS' 1ST COMING

"He shall be great, and shall be called the Son of the Highest: and the Lord God shall give unto him the throne of his father David: And he shall reign over the house of Jacob for ever; and of his kingdom there shall be no end."

Luke 1:32-33

The Story Line

In eternity past, God's plan for the climax of His story was to be when He became a human in Jesus Christ. God became a human to redeem people from the curse of sin, and offer them eternal life. When mankind rebelled against God by breaking His law, God in His justice had to be faithful to the eternal laws which are part of His pure, holy kingdom. That meant that after man died physically he would have to be eternally separated from God because God is perfect and can not have fellowship with anyone who is not perfect too. Therefore, God chose to come into the world He created to defeat the curse of sin, so that men could be made right with their Creator once again!

Jesus' Birth

The Author of Life chose to begin His earthly life the same way we begin ours, except for one major difference: He would be born of a virgin! Unlike any other pregnancy, this one would be divinely unique. The anticipation of a coming Savior was the hope of all Israel. The prophet Nathan had predicted this heavenly event, and the people cried to God, their eternal King, to come save them (2 Sa 7:4-17). At the time appointed, God handpicked a young Israelite woman to carry earth's most precious infant. He sent His angel, Gabriel, to impart to her this monumental news. The glad announcement was wonderful but also alarmingly frightful. She was engaged and not to be wed for many months, Who would believe her miraculous pregnancy story? When her espoused husband, Joseph, discovered his fiancee was with child, he imagined she had been unfaithful and broken their engagement vow. As Joseph thought on these things with a heavy heart, he decided to call off the marriage, but the Lord spoke to him in a dream through Gabriel, His messenger. God revealed to Joseph that his soon-to-be wife had conceived, not of man, but of the Holy Spirit and he should not be afraid to take her as his wife, for she carried in her womb the Savior of sinners. Joseph was instructed in his dream to call this Divine Child, Jesus! Joseph awoke with God's revelation in his heart and obeyed the angel's directions, taking to wife his betrothed, Mary (Mt 1:18-25).

The theological name for the impregnation of God's Son into Mary's womb is called the incarnation, that is, the moment of conception when God, the Creator of the heaven's and the earth, put on human flesh in a women's womb. In God's human state He was fully human and fully God. The incarnation is a mind blowing time in history which began the climax of The Lord's story, but the peak of the climax is still to come! Most everyone who processes the incarnation usually asks themselves, How is that possible? The answer is simple: The One True God who created everything has the power!

When the incarnation began, God's Spirit caused the young Israelite woman to become pregnant. Nine months later the world was never the same! When the time in human history was right, when the stage was properly set, God breathed His first breath in the flesh as a babe. The Old Testament Scriptures foretold this would happen hundreds of years in advance, even down to very specific details. For example, God's prophet Isaiah uttered the following words, *"Therefore the Lord himself shall give you a sign; Behold, a virgin shall conceive, and bear a son, and shall call his name Immanuel [God with us]" (Is 7:14).* Again, God later spoke through Isaiah saying, *"For unto us a child is born, unto us a son is given: and the government shall be upon his shoulder: and his name shall be called Wonderful, Counsellor, The mighty God, The everlasting Father, The Prince of Peace" (Is 9:6).* Isaiah's precise prophecies informed Israel a virgin would bear God Himself into the world, and all these names would be used to describe Him. The prophet Nathan informed Israel Jesus would descend from the family line of King David (2 Sa 7:4-17). (For more information about Jesus' prophetic genealogical record, please read Appendix III on page 203.) To remove all doubt, The Lord even gave the geographic location of where He was to be born. Consider the following verse from the prophet Micah: *"But thou, Bethlehem Ephratah, though thou be little among the thousands of Judah, yet out of thee shall he come forth unto me that is to be ruler in Israel; whose goings forth have been from of old, from everlasting" (Mi 5:2).* Micah's prophecy was proven true when Jesus was born in Bethlehem as the Scriptures record (Mt 2; Lk 2). Although neither Mary nor Joseph lived in Bethlehem, it was Joseph's ancestral home. Living in Nazareth, they lived almost 100 miles to the north. [69] But this was not an obstacle for God. God used an act of the government to get Joseph and Mary to the appointed place where the Messiah was to be born. Quite unexpectedly, the current ruling power (Rome) demanded a census be taken of all the known world so a tax could be issued. The census required everyone to go back to their ancestral homes. This meant Joseph and his very pregnant wife had to travel all those miles across the barren lands of Israel. Upon arrival, they found the city overflowing with people and were unable to find lodging anywhere. The only place found available was where livestock was kept, probably a stable or small cave. **On that night, the Creator of Life was born into the world He had spoken into existence!** The Bible says His mother laid her newborn Son in a manger (a grain bin used to feed animals). On the evening of His birth, God announced the eternally significant miracle in the night sky to some lowly shepherds through an angel. At the sudden appearance of this bright heavenly being the shepherds quaked in fear. The angel of the Lord said to them,

> *...Fear not: for, behold, I bring you good tidings of great joy, which shall be to all people. For unto you is born this day in the city of David a Saviour, which is Christ the Lord. And this shall be a sign unto you; Ye shall find the babe wrapped in swaddling clothes, lying in a manger. And suddenly there was with the angel a multitude of the heavenly host praising God, and saying, Glory to God in the highest, and on earth peace, good will toward men.*

Luke 2:10-14

Then God lit up the sky that night with a host of angels giving glory at the Savior's birth! As the glorious light faded away, the shepherds said one to another, *"...Let us now go even unto Bethlehem, and see this thing which is come to pass, which the Lord hath made known unto us"* (Lk 2:15). The Bible tells us these men hurried to Bethlehem and found Joseph and Mary, as well as, the Savior of the world lying in a manger as the angels had said! Once their eyes had beheld this prophetic Child, the shepherds excitedly spread the news to many about everything they had witnessed! Later that evening, *"...the shepherds returned, glorifying and praising God for all the things that they had heard and seen, as it was told unto them"* (Lk 2:20).

According to the law God had given His people through Moses, Joseph and Mary were to offer a sacrifice at the temple for their first born, signifying they were dedicating Him to God (Ex 13:2). Also, eight days after His birth they were to have the child circumcised, in accordance with God's law. (Not surprisingly, modern science confirms that after a child is eight days old they begin to produce sufficient amounts of vitamin k, which allows for blood clotting, so the eighth day is the safest day to perform the circumcision surgery.[70]) While Joseph and Mary were at the temple performing their responsibilities to the Lord, they experienced two divine encounters, confirming to them their Son was indeed the Christ Child, the long awaited Messiah. Their first encounter was with a righteous man named Simeon. Simeon had been promised by the Lord he would not die until his eyes beheld the coming Messiah. Since then, he had been waiting in anticipation for the fulfillment of this promise. On that day when the infant Savior was in the temple, the Spirit of God came upon Simeon, leading him to the child where

> ...he [took] him up in his arms, and blessed God, and said, Lord, now lettest thou thy servant depart in peace, according to thy word: For mine eyes have seen thy salvation, Which thou hast prepared before the face of all people; A light to lighten the Gentiles, and the glory of thy people Israel.

> *Luke 2:28-32*

Simeon blessed Joseph and Mary, and continued saying, *"Behold, this child is set for the fall and rising again of many in Israel; and for a sign which shall be spoken against; (Yea, a sword shall pierce through thy own soul also,) that the thoughts of many hearts may be revealed" (Lk 2:34-35).* This man's prophetic words amazed Jesus' parents. The second divine encounter happened just as Simeon was finishing his declaration. An elderly prophetess named Anna was passing by and upon seeing the babe she began voicing thanks aloud in the temple for the Messiah's appearing! The Bible says she *"[spoke] of him to all them that looked for redemption in Jerusalem" (Lk 2:38).*

During the first eight days of His life in the flesh, The Lord confirmed to Joseph and Mary their Son was the eternal King of all Creation. He used the shepherds, Simeon, and Anna to comfort and assure them of His promise during a time of hardship and change in their lives. About a year or so after Jesus had been born, the evidence of yet another confirmation was sent to this small family which had been recorded in the stars (Mt 2). Although not everyone understood astrological signs in the heaven's, there were a few wise men in the East whose eyes had been pointed upwards when this Miracle Child was born. These men perceived God's hand at work through a star signifying the King of all kings had made His entrance into the world. Without delay, the men decided to take gifts to their King, so they followed the star to the seemingly insignificant town of Bethlehem. When they finally arrived and saw Jesus they *"...fell down, and worshipped him: and when they had opened their treasures, they presented unto him gifts; gold, and frankincense and myrrh" (Mt 2:11).* **These gifts honored the God of Glory who had put on flesh, perfectly fulfilling His incarnation prophecies. His birth was celebrated in the heavens and announced to the world! The God of Abraham, Isaac, and Jacob now walked the earth, and it would never be the same!**

Jesus' Pre-Ministry Life

The first years of Jesus' life ushered excitement and change into the lives of His newly wed parents. Their adventure continued soon after the wise men left to return to their own country. The Lord appeared to Joseph in a dream saying, *"...Arise, and take the young child and his mother, and flee into Egypt, and be thou there until I bring thee word: for Herod will seek the young child to destroy him" (Lk 2:13).*

Herod was a wicked ruler in the land of Israel, who learned from the wise men the King of the Jews had been born. When he heard this news, jealous fury seized him! Herod commanded all children, two years old and under, living in or around Bethlehem be killed! This monstrous ruler hoped to ensure this baby would never become king and threaten his throne. Herod's plans to destroy the Promised Child did not succeed, for Joseph heeded the dream the Lord had given him and escaped the ruthless slaughter. Once Herod died, the Lord appeared to Joseph in another dream and told him Herod was dead, and it was now safe for them to return to Israel. Joseph took his wife and their child back to his home, where it had all began, the town of Nazareth (Lk 1:26; 2:39).

Not much is recorded in the Bible about Jesus' childhood except for one event in *Luke 2:41-52*. It was Passover and Jesus' parents traveled to Jerusalem for the festival, as they did each year. If you remember, this festival was to commemorate how the death angel had passed over the Israelites during the 10th plague in Egypt. When the celebration was over Jesus' parents began their long journey (80+ miles) back to Nazareth with a group of their companions who had also gone to celebrate.[71] What Jesus' parents didn't know was that their Son had not joined their company, but had stayed behind in Jerusalem. A full day of travel had gone by before they discovered He was missing! Panicked and worried they rushed back to find their young boy. After three days of searching, they finally found Jesus in the temple, where He was:

> *...sitting in the midst of the doctors, both hearing them, and asking them questions. And all that heard him were astonished at his understanding and answers. And when they saw him, they were amazed: and his mother said unto him, Son, why hast thou thus dealt with us? behold, thy father and I have sought thee sorrowing. And he said unto them, How is it that ye sought me? wist ye not that I must be about my Father's business? And they understood not the saying which he spake [spoke] unto them.*

Luke 2:46-50

No one knows what young Jesus said in His conversations with these educated men (who were most likely temple priests), but whatever it was we know it glorified God and taught truth, since He answered His parents saying, *"I must be about my Father's business."* When Jesus' parents heard His response, they were perplexed and didn't fully understand, even though it had been revealed to them years earlier He was the promised Savior of sinners. This is the last event in Jesus' childhood the Scriptures record for us before He begins His earthly, professional ministry.

Jesus' Ministry

Six months before Jesus' birth, Mary's cousin Elizabeth and her husband Zachariah gave birth to a very special young boy named John. John's birth was another of God's wonder-working stories that was foretold to his father by the angel Gabriel, and he was to have a unique and special mission when he grew up. John was to be the forerunner of the Savior. In the natural world kings have people who go ahead of them to announce their coming. Likewise, John was the forerunner of Jesus, The King of all Creation, announcing His coming to the people of Israel. John proclaimed the coming of Christ by preaching *"...Repent, for the kingdom of heaven has come near" (Mt 3:1).* At this time John was living in the wilderness and baptizing people in the Jordan river. He would baptize (baptism is discussed in more detail on page 160) those who desired to display their repentance and faith in God publicly. When Jesus was ready to begin His public ministry He made His way to the river where John was preaching. As John's eyes looked up and saw Jesus approaching him he said,

> *...Behold the Lamb of God, which taketh away the sin of the world. This is he of whom I said, After me cometh a man which is preferred before me: for he was before me.*

And I knew him not: but that he should be made manifest
to Israel, therefore am I come baptizing with water
John 1:29-31

His words affirmed Jesus was the long awaited Messiah Israel had prayed for, and He would restore man's broken relationship with God. As John ended his words, Jesus moved closer to be baptized by him. Taken back, John refused, but Jesus insisted he must baptize Him, in order to fulfill God's perfect plan. Out of the four gospels (*Matthew, Mark, Luke* and *John*), the book of *Mark* records what happened next with the most detail. The Bible says John baptized Jesus and then as He rose out of the water *"...he saw the heavens opened, and the Spirit like a dove descending upon him: And there came a voice from heaven, saying, Thou art my beloved Son, in whom I am well pleased" (Mk 1:10-11).* This powerful passage marked the beginning of Jesus' ministry, highlighting the Triune nature of the One True Eternal God who had spoken in times past to Adam and later to Abraham all those years ago.

The God of the Bible, of all creation, is a Triune God! Meaning, He is One God, who is Three Persons. We see the Trinity clearly in Jesus' baptism. The voice speaking *"Thou art my beloved Son"* is God the Father. Jesus is God the Son. The Spirit who descended on the Son is God the Spirit (Mk 1:10-11). The Trinity is difficult for people to understand, but the Scriptures are clear God is One in Three and Three in One. The following quote from the president of ICR, Henry Morris III, has been included to help provide a little more insight into the doctrine of the Trinity.

> God is the infinite, invisible, omnipresent Father of all. But He is also the Son, who is visible and touchable and yet the perfectly holy Word who is always revealing and manifesting the Father. And God is also the Holy Spirit, always present to guide, convict, and comfort. A majestic mystery, but a wonderful reality! Three divine persons, each equally

and totally God. We can not adequately compre-
hend this reality with our finite minds, but we are
compelled to acknowledge it and believe it and rejoice in our hearts.[72]

Jesus' ministry lasted for three to three and a half years. Throughout
His ministry He did great deeds. For our purposes, *The Gospel Octagon* will highlight four key areas of Jesus' earthly ministry: Jesus
the Healer, Jesus the Teacher, Jesus the Disciple Maker, and Jesus
the Prophet.

Jesus, the Healer

One of the major parts, or at least the most memorable por-
tions of Jesus' ministry was the power He employed as He healed
those in need. Jesus healed a variety of inflicted people, such as, the
sick, the demon possessed, the blind, the lame, and most amazingly
the dead. His healing works were a fulfillment of the prophecies
spoken of Him by the prophets many years prior. For example,
Isaiah wrote, *"...the eyes of the blind shall be opened, and the ears of the
deaf shall be unstopped. Then shall the lame man leap as an hart, and the
tongue of the dumb sing..." (Is 43:5-6).* The first recorded healing miracle in the New Testament is found in *Matthew* 8, where Jesus
healed a man with leprosy, a deadly contagious skin disease. The
Bible tells us the infected man came near Jesus and worshipped
Him saying, *"Lord, if thou wilt, thou canst [can] make me clean" (Mt
8:2).* Jesus touched the man and responded, *"I will; be thou clean"
(Mt 8:3).* As He spoke, the man was cleansed! This was the first of
many healing miracles Jesus performed during the few years of His
earthly ministry (Jn 21:25). Continuing on in both the eighth and
ninth chapter of *Matthew* we find Jesus healed the paralyzed. Both
passages reveal **faith in Jesus is the key to being healed.** As
well, both passages show it is not the inflicted individual who had
faith, but their friend's faith that Jesus honors. In the latter of the

two passages, Jesus used the healing miracle to testify He was God.
The Scriptures read,

> ...behold, they brought to him a man sick of the palsy
> [lame], lying on a bed: and Jesus seeing their faith said
> unto the sick of the palsy; Son, be of good cheer; thy sins
> be forgiven thee. And, behold, certain of the scribes said
> within themselves, This man blasphemeth. And Jesus
> knowing their thoughts said, Wherefore think ye evil in
> your hearts? For whether is easier, to say, Thy sins be
> forgiven thee; or to say, Arise, and walk? But that ye may
> know that the Son of man hath power on earth to forgive
> sins, (then saith he to the sick of the palsy,) Arise, take up
> thy bed, and go unto thine house. And he arose, and de-
> parted to his house. But when the multitudes saw it, they
> marvelled, and glorified God, which had given such
> power unto men.

Matthew 9:2-8

Here we see Jesus healed the lame man because of his friends' faith.
Prior to the healing Jesus told the man his sins are forgiven. This
was something only God could do, as the Israelites well knew. **Jesus
is God and He alone has the power to forgive man's sins**
(Jn 14:6; Ac 4:12). Therefore Jesus said,

> For whether is easier, to say, Thy sins be forgiven thee;
> or to say, Arise, and walk? But that ye may know that the
> Son of man hath power on earth to forgive sins, (then
> saith he to the sick of the palsy,) Arise, take up thy bed,
> and go unto thine house.

Matthew 9:5-6

The next portion of Scripture goes on to tell us that this once lame
man walked away! His crippled body was given new life by God
Himself! Another very important point in this story is that Jesus
calls Himself the *Son of Man*. This title has great significance, for
Jesus is referring to a prophetic passage from the book of *Daniel*.
Daniel was one of God's prophets who had lived most of his life in
Babylon because the Babylonians had conquered and taken captive

the Israelites during his life. Even though the land of Israel had been conquered during Daniel's lifetime, God still spoke through prophets to His people. Daniel had a handful of miraculous encounters with the Lord. In one of those encounters God had given Daniel a vision which revealed Himself in the form of a human. This descriptive passage is in *Daniel* 7, and Jesus was referencing it every time He used the title, *Son of man*. Daniel's words are recorded in the following vision:

> *I saw in the night visions, and, behold, one like the **Son of man** came with the clouds of heaven, and came to the Ancient of days, and they brought him near before him. And there was given him dominion, and glory, and a kingdom, that all people, nations, and languages, should serve him: his dominion is an everlasting dominion, which shall not pass away, and his kingdom that which shall not be destroyed.*

> *Daniel 7:13-14*

In this vision Daniel saw a figure in the clouds having a divine, yet, human appearance coming near the *Ancient of days,* who is God the Father. Daniel witnessed God the Father give His Son sovereignty over everything for all time and into eternity. This passage is very important in understanding Jesus' ministry because Jesus is giving Himself this powerful title, *Son of man*. Jesus is saying He is the Son of man from this passage in *Daniel*. And when Jesus gave Himself this title, the Hebrews knew He was saying, *"I am God! I am the One who will receive a Kingdom that will last forever, and I will rule everyone and everything, for all things belong to Me!"* Throughout Jesus' ministry He continued to heal people and use this title, and the religious leaders increasingly grew in hatred for Him. They thought the usage of His self-given title was blasphemy, and it would've been if Jesus was not truly God, but HE IS!

Later in His ministry, Jesus was traveling by boat with His disciples to the Geransenes region. As they were pulling up on shore, they were suddenly confronted by a man who was possessed by many demons. The man was violent and uncontrollable so he'd been cast out of the community. He was now dwelling among the dead in the cemetery. The demons within him would cause him to howl like an animal and cut his body. When the tormented man saw Jesus the Bible records,

> *...he ran and worshipped him, And cried with a loud voice, and said, What have I to do with thee, Jesus, thou Son of the most high God? I adjure thee by God, that thou torment me not. For he said unto him, Come out of the man, thou unclean spirit. And he asked him, What is thy name? And he answered, saying, My name is Legion: for we are many. And he besought him much that he would not send them away out of the country. Now there was there nigh unto the mountains a great herd of swine feeding. And all the devils besought him, saying, Send us into the swine, that we may enter into them. And forthwith Jesus gave them leave. And the unclean spirits went out, and entered into the swine: and the herd ran violently down a steep place into the sea, (they were about two thousand;) and were choked in the sea.*

Mark 5:6-13

Interestingly, the demons inside the possessed man recognized immediately Jesus was the Son of God. These evil workers of Satan were the ones controlling this man's actions, causing him to be violent, out of control, and self destructive in cutting himself. The demons were much afraid and begged Jesus not to torment them, for they knew the authority He carried. At one time these demons had dwelt with Jesus in His kingdom as heavenly angels before wickedly joining Satan in his sinful rebellion. (Please reference page 56.) Their evil choices caused them to be banished from God's kingdom and these angels are now demons assisting Satan in his dark and vile workings among the children of men. These demons possessing the tormented man were very aware of the power Jesus held as King and Lord of all, and they must obey His bidding. Jesus sent the demons into the herd of swine, casting them out of the man and healing him from demonic possession. After this, the story continues:

> *And they that fed the swine fled, and told it in the city, and in the country. And they went out to see what it was that was done. And they come to Jesus, and see him that was possessed with the devil, and had the legion, sitting, and clothed, and in his right mind: and they were afraid. And they that saw it told them how it befell to him that was possessed with the devil, and also concerning the swine. And they began to pray him to depart out of their coasts. And when he was come into the ship, he that had been possessed with the devil prayed him that he might be with him. Howbeit Jesus suffered him not, but saith unto him, Go home to thy friends, and tell them how great things the Lord hath done for thee, and hath had compassion on thee. And he departed, and began to pub-lish [declare] in Decapolis how great things Jesus had done for him: and all men did marvel.*

Mark 5:14-20

Fear swept over the pig herdsmen. They ran to the city and told everyone what had occurred. Instead of rejoicing that the dangerous, crazy man was now clothed and in his right mind, the towns people were greatly disturbed and upset that their pig business had been ruined! Disregarding this life changing miracle, they asked Jesus to leave! But, the man delivered from demon possession pursued after Jesus and asked if he could follow Him. Jesus charged the man to stay in his town to be a witness and light of the miracle God had done in his life. The man was faithful in this, and even traveled around the region telling others about the healing power of God.

The healing ministry of Jesus seems to have four primary purposes. One, to show Jesus was God. Two, to show God has the authority to forgive sins. Three, to show God's love and compassion. Four, to show that faith is intricately connected to one's relationship with God. The healing hands of Jesus were often used as a platform for His teaching ministry.

Jesus, the Teacher

On the Mountain of Sinai God presented to Moses with laws for His people, but since that time the hearts of the Israelite people would often stray from God's instructions for life. The Lord spoke through His prophets to remind them to obey His law. Different religious teachers rose up, some speaking truth and others uttering untruth, leading many astray. When Jesus came to the earth He was not interested in popular opinion, but teaching the solid truth of God's Word. This was a big part of His mission, for He is the Truth (Jn 14:6)!

The most famous teaching of Jesus is found in the book of *Matthew*, and is three chapters long. This teaching is a complete sermon Jesus delivered on a large hillside. The message has been called *The Sermon on the Mount*. Jesus' words were focused on living for God. He began His message by explaining what kind of attitude would bring the blessing of God. Here is a section of it in the following passage of Scripture:

> *Blessed are the poor in spirit: for theirs is the kingdom of heaven. Blessed are they that mourn: for they shall be comforted. Blessed are the meek: for they shall inherit the earth. Blessed are they which do hunger and thirst after righteousness: for they shall be filled. Blessed are the merciful: for they shall obtain mercy. Blessed are the pure in heart: for they shall see God. Blessed are the peacemakers: for they shall be called the children of God. Blessed are they which are persecuted for righteousness' sake: for theirs is the kingdom of heaven. Blessed are ye, when men shall revile you, and persecute you, and shall say all manner of evil against you falsely, for my sake. Rejoice, and be exceeding glad: for great is your reward in heaven: for so persecuted they the prophets which were before you.*

Matthew 5:3-12

Here Jesus provides eight attitudes every person who is following after God should possess or strive towards. He starts each of them off by saying *"Blessed."* This word means *happy*. For example, Jesus said, *"Blessed are the poor in spirit...,"* which means, those who are poor in spirit will be happy (Mt 5:3)! Let's take a look at how Jesus began His sermon by reviewing these eight beatitudes:

1. **Poor in spirit** means that one recognizes their spiritual poverty apart from God. They recognize their need for God in their life due to the separation that sin has caused.

2. **Mourn** speaks of one who is mourning or sorrowful because of their sin or the sins of the world.

3. **Meek** means to be humble and having strength under control.

4. **Hunger and thirst after righteousness** means one who is eager to seek God.

5. **Merciful** means those who extend compassion, and forgiveness to others when they fall short of God's standard of perfection and/or to those who have been affected by the sinfulness of this world.

6. **Pure in heart** means those who desire to abstain from sin and repent (turn from) from sin, when they fall into it, living obediently toward God.

7. **Peacemakers** are those who desire to bring peace into situations without compromising on truth.

8. **Persecuted for righteousness** speaks of one who stands up for the truth and is persecuted.

Jesus began His sermon by presenting these eight attitudes and assuring you will be blessed or *happy* if you live according to this overview. Interestingly, He expounds on the last one, saying if Christ followers are persecuted for their faith then we should rejoice! What!? Why would anyone want to rejoice in persecution? God promises those who are persecuted will have a great reward in the Kingdom of Heaven, for in like manner God's prophets were persecuted.

Many of the subjects Jesus teaches on in this sermon focuses on providing the correct meaning of a law or action God's children should follow, opposed to some of the false teachings the Israelites were being taught from their religious teachers. Regarding adultery, it was taught Jews didn't actually commit adultery until they committed the physical action. Jesus exposed this to be a lie and taught them the truth saying, *"Ye have heard that it was said by them of old time, Thou shalt not commit adultery: But I say unto you, That whosoever looketh on a woman to lust after her hath committed adultery with her already in his heart" (Mt 5:27-30).* First, Jesus reminds His hearers of the seventh commandment, which they all knew well. Then, He continued with, *"But I say unto you."* In other words, Jesus was saying, *"I am God. I am the One who first spoke this commandment to your forefathers from the top of Mount Sinai. This is what the commandment originally intended, but ungodly men have distorted my words to rationalize and please their wicked sin nature."* Jesus took five other commands given to Moses, uncovered false teaching about them and then provided the proper, God-intended meaning. These are each addressed in the fifth chapter of *Matthew.*

In the very next chapter, *Matthew* 6 Jesus evoked further corrections. He declared there are people in Israel, even leaders, who were hypocrites. He then provided three examples of their hypocritical actions, explaining how to truly be obedient to God. Jesus exposed how people are hypocritical with their financial giving, praying, and fasting. He said hypocrites contribute offerings in a public manner so everyone will see, they pray long, wordy prayers on the street corner so everyone will hear, and they fast with a distorted, somber face so everyone will know how sacrificially faithful

they are to God. Jesus verbally corrected their foolish ways. He affirmed all three of these actions are good, but not to do them like
hypocrites. Rather, Jesus encouraged financial giving to be done
privately. He said, *"...let not thy left hand know what thy right hand doeth: That thine alms may be in secret: and thy Father which seeth in secret
himself shall reward thee openly" (Mt 6:3-4)*. Regarding prayer, Jesus
taught God's children to pray in private and not use *"...vain repeti-
tions, as the heathen do..." (Mt 6:7)*. Next, Jesus taught when you fast
to do so in secret, so only God knows. When teaching about these
topics He assured both the hypocrite and the one humbly following
God would receive a reward. The reward for the hypocrite would
simply be the applause of men. But, the reward for those following
Jesus' Word would last forever in the Kingdom of Heaven (Mt 6:4,
6, 18).

To close *The Sermon on the Mount,* Jesus taught about true
and false believers. Jesus began by teaching there were only two
gates every person in the world could choose to go through in their
life, without regards to their position in the world. The one gate has
a broad road leading to hell. The other gate has a narrow road leading to heaven. Jesus explained many go the way of the broad road
and a small number of people go down the narrow road. Next, Jesus
taught there were two types of people who *claimed* to be going down
the narrow road. He said some were liars and some spoke truthfully.
The wisdom of His words revealed there is a key to identify which is
which. He used symbolism by comparing people to trees, and what
comes out of people to a tree's fruit. Jesus said, *"Wherefore by their
fruits ye shall know them" (Mt 7:20)*. In other words, Jesus was saying
people's words and actions reveal whether their confession to be
following the One, True God is true or false. As one can identify a
tree by its fruit, likewise one should be able to identify a person by
their fruit. After revealing this, Jesus declared a day of judgement is
coming when He will judge between the true and false believers:

*Not every one that saith unto me, Lord, Lord, shall enter
into the kingdom of heaven; but he that doeth the will of
my Father which is in heaven. Many will say to me in
that day, Lord, Lord, have we not prophesied in thy
name? and in thy name have cast out devils? and in thy
name done many wonderful works? And then will I profess unto them, I never knew you: depart from me, ye that
work iniquity.*

Matthew 7:21-23

This passage of Scripture is frightening. God is saying there are
some people who profess Jesus to be Lord, but He does not even
know them! He has no relationship with them. Their sins have not
been forgiven, even though they believe they have. The people Jesus
is describing are either liars or they have been severely deceived by
Satan. To consider the later of these two scenarios is a terrifying
thought.

Jesus finished His sermon by explaining there are two
foundations people will build their lives on: the rock (truth: God's
Word) or the sand (lies: man's word). He compared those who listen
and obey His teaching to be like those who build their house on a
rock. When the storms rage their house will stand firm. In the same
manner, those who do not obey His teachings are like a foolish man
who builds his house on sand. When the storms rage their house will
collapse with a great crash (Mt 7:24-27). When Jesus finished this
sermon *"the people were astonished at his doctrine: For he taught them
as one having authority, and not as the scribes" (Mt 7:28-29).* Jesus truly
taught with authority, unlike any other man on earth.

Jesus was the Master of all teachers who had or will ever
live. He would often convey His lessons and teachings through stories called parables. Parables were stories, sometimes allegorical,
which used the common circumstances and objects of the day to
help people better understand spiritual truths.[73] The *Baker Ency-*

clopedia of the Bible calculated that 35 percent of Jesus' sayings
were parables. Here is one of Jesus' parables about a farmer sowing
seed. Jesus began His story saying,

> *...Behold, a sower went forth to sow; And when he
> sowed, some seeds fell by the way side, and the fowls
> came and devoured them up: Some fell upon stony
> places, where they had not much earth: and forthwith
> they sprung up, because they had no deepness of earth:
> And when the sun was up, they were scorched; and be-
> cause they had no root, they withered away. And some
> fell among thorns; and the thorns sprung up, and choked
> them: But other fell into good ground, and brought forth
> fruit, some an hundredfold, some sixtyfold, some thirty-
> fold. Who hath ears to hear, let him hear.*
>
> Matthew 13:3-9

Jesus was the Creator of speech, making Him masterfully skilled in
communicating His truths to any type of person. For this parable,
Jesus was speaking to the common, every-day farmers, shepherds,
and fishermen. He used their type of lingo so they could compre-
hend His meaning. When Jesus spoke about agriculture in this
story, they understood! Shortly after telling the parable, Jesus unfolded its symbolism.

> *Hear ye therefore the parable of the sower. When any
> one heareth the word of the kingdom, and understandeth
> it not, then cometh the wicked one, and catcheth away
> that which was sown in his heart. This is he which re-
> ceived seed by the way side. But he that received the seed
> into stony places, the same is he that heareth the word,
> and anon [at once] with joy receiveth it; Yet hath he not
> root in himself, but [en]dureth for a while: for when
> tribulation or persecution ariseth because of the word,
> by and by he is offended. He also that received seed
> among the thorns is he that heareth the word; and the
> care of this world, and the deceitfulness of riches, choke
> the word, and he becometh unfruitful. But he that re-
> ceived seed into the good ground is he that heareth the
> word, and understandeth it; which also beareth fruit, and*

bringeth forth, some an hundredfold, some sixty, some thirty.

Matthew 13:18-23

Jesus explained how the farmer sowing seed describes God sowing the Gospel truth into the lives of four different types of people. One heard the Gospel and rejected God immediately. Two others believed the Gospel but after some time turned their backs on God. The last one received the Gospel and obeyed God with great joy in His heart, sharing with others the Gospel truth!

Jesus would also tell parables and *not* explain their hidden meanings. One such parable went like this, *"the kingdom of heaven is like unto treasure hid in a field; the which when a man hath found, he hideth, and for joy thereof goeth and selleth all that he hath, and buyeth that field" (Mt 13:44).* Although Jesus did not provide a detailed explanation, if you compare it to the other parables He had explained, and pair it with the Bible's full story, it's not so difficult to deduce. The treasure in this story represents the truth of God's Kingdom which must be found. The man found the treasure (truth) about God and gave up everything he owned to buy the treasure. In other words, God is saying people who truly desire to be in His Kingdom will seek for Him as though seeking for valuable treasure, and when they find Him, they give up everything else the world offers to devote themselves fully to God's truth.

Jesus taught another parable without explaining its meaning but also is easy enough to decipher. The parable goes, *"the kingdom of heaven is like unto a merchant man, seeking goodly pearls: Who, when he had found one pearl of great price, went and sold all that he had, and bought it" (Mt 13:45-46).* In this parable, the merchant man represents Jesus. He is seeking goodly pearls, which represent people who desire/need Him. God sacrificed all He had to purchase them.

Jesus was prophesying about how He had given up everything to put on flesh so He could die on a cross to break the curse of man's sin. Through the cross, God would redeem spiritually dead men by giving them eternal life!

Another key area Jesus taught about was the end times or what is sometimes called the end of the human age. Jesus is the Author of His story and He wanted mankind to be informed and knowledgeable about the end of this earthly age. (The end times will be discussed in greater detail in chapter six.) He desired as many people as possible would repent of their sins and put their faith in Him for the forgiveness of their sins before they passed into eternity. **Jesus spent much of His time on earth teaching His disciples so they would continue to teach the truth of God's Word after His earthly ministry was complete.**

Jesus, the Disciple Maker

Jesus healed those in need, and preached to thousands. In addition to healing and preaching, another significant part of His focus was training and teaching His disciples. According to *The Baker Encyclopedia of the Bible*, a disciple is "Someone who follows another person or another way of life and who submits himself to the discipline (teaching) of that leader or way."[74] Directly after Jesus was baptized, He set about choosing 12 men whom He would mentor and use to change the world! Scripture recounts,

> *Jesus, walking by the sea of Galilee, saw two brethren, Simon called Peter, and Andrew his brother, casting a net into the sea: for they were fishers. And he saith unto them, Follow me, and I will make you fishers of men. And they straightway left their nets, and followed him.*

> *Matthew 4:18-20*

Jesus desired to turn these fishermen into men who would "fish" for the souls of men! Jesus had more than 12 disciples, for all were and are welcome to follow Him, but these 12 He handpicked to fulfill a special purpose. The 12 were intimately close to the Lord during His few years of earthly ministry. They were able to learn from Jesus when the crowds would dissipate. They could ask questions about Jesus' teaching or any other matter that came to mind. For example, Jesus taught the following parable to a crowd of people:

> *The kingdom of heaven is likened unto a man which*
> *sowed good seed in his field: But while men slept, his*
> *enemy came and sowed tares among the wheat, and went*
> *his way. But when the blade was sprung up, and brought*
> *forth fruit, then appeared the tares also. So the servants*
> *of the householder came and said unto him, Sir, didst not*
> *thou sow good seed in thy field? from whence then hath*
> *it tares? He said unto them, An enemy hath done this.*
> *The servants said unto him, Wilt thou then that we go*
> *and gather them up? But he said, Nay; lest while ye*
> *gather up the tares, ye root up also the wheat with them.*
> *Let both grow together until the harvest: and in the time*
> *of harvest I will say to the reapers, Gather ye together*
> *first the tares, and bind them in bundles to burn them:*
> *but gather the wheat into my barn.*

Matthew 13:24-30

When Jesus finished telling this parable He continued teaching on other things. The Bible tells us after Jesus and His disciples had left the crowds, the 12 inquired after the meaning behind this particular parable since He had not provided an explanation. Jesus obliged their question, providing the following answer:

> *...He that soweth the good seed is the Son of man; The*
> *field is the world; the good seed are the children of the*
> *kingdom; but the tares are the children of the wicked*
> *one; The enemy that sowed them is the devil; the harvest*
> *is the end of the world; and the reapers are the angels.*
> *As therefore the tares are gathered and burned in the*
> *fire; so shall it be in the end of this world. The Son of*
> *man shall send forth his angels, and they shall gather out*
> *of his kingdom all things that offend, and them which do*
> *iniquity; And shall cast them into a furnace of fire: there*
> *shall be wailing and gnashing of teeth. Then shall the*

*righteous shine forth as the sun in the kingdom of their
Father. Who hath ears to hear, let him hear.*

Matthew 13:37-43

Being one of the hand picked disciples of Christ must have been
wonderful, for they had the incredible blessing of learning from and
walking with God Himself. However, this immense privilege
brought with it great responsibility.

During His ministry on earth, Jesus spent a vast majority of
His time healing, teaching, and discipling the Israelite people, for
that was His purpose: they are the nation God specifically created
for Himself. Yet, God had a *bigger purpose* in mind than just teaching the Israelites to know Him. **Jesus focused on discipling the
12 so they would go into the world and share the Gospel at
His appointed time with any and all who would listen.**

Jesus, the Prophet

Earlier in chapter three we learned a prophet is a person
whom God uses to speak to people, especially the Israelites. When
God came to the earth He became the ultimate Prophet! Being in
human form, He was now His own mouth piece! While Jesus was on
the earth He prophesied about many future events, including: the
church, His death and resurrection, and the end times and His 2nd
coming.

To begin, Jesus prophesied about the church. Jesus had
come to His people, the Israelites (Mt 15:24), but His earthly mission consisted of a much greater purpose which would include the
whole world and not just the Hebrews. He came to bring a new
covenant to the earth, and spread His truth through those who proclaim Him as Christ and follow after His teachings, His church. In
eternity past, God intended that the church would spread the Gospel

and bear the LIGHT OF TRUTH to the world. One day as Jesus was
teaching the Israelites, He likened Himself to a shepherd who cared
for His sheep (Israel). He went on prophesying, *"And other sheep I
have, which are not of this fold: them also I must bring, and they shall hear
my voice; and there shall be one fold, and one shepherd" (Jn 10:16)*. Jesus' words indicated His bigger plan. Not only would the truths and
promises He spoke of be for the Israelites, but also for the entire
world, to anyone who desired to follow Him and His words of eternal truth.

Secondly, Jesus prophesied about His death and resurrection. One day Jesus asked His disciples privately who people
thought He was. They responded that some believed He was Elijah,
the prophet from days long ago, and others said He was John the
Baptist (Jesus' cousin), raised from the dead (Mk 8:27-28)! After
hearing their answers, He put the question to them, and asked,
"...But whom say ye that I am" (Mk 8:29)? At this, the disciple named
Peter answered and said, *"Thou art the Christ" (Mk 8:29)*. The word
Christ is a Greek word which means savior. Peter's declaration was
true, but for the time being, Jesus instructed them not to tell anyone. Because of the words of the prophets, the Israelites believed
God was going to send them a Savior to deliver them from the bonds
of their enemies. They did not *fully* understand God's story, however. Even those closest to Jesus did not grasp the fullness of the
plan and story He was unraveling, and His role as Savior. Jesus
hadn't come to the earth to deliver them from their enemies, at least
not yet. God's plan and promise for deliverance would indeed be
fulfilled, but not in the way the Israelites had supposed. After Jesus
instructed His disciples not to reveal He was the Christ, He went on
and disclosed to them, *"...the Son of man must suffer many things, and
be rejected of the elders, and of the chief priests, and scribes, and be killed,
and after three days rise again" (Mk 8:31)*. Immediately after Jesus
spoke these words, Peter wrongly rebuked Jesus saying His proph-

ecy would not come true (Mk 8:32; Mt 16:22). To which Jesus responded by rightly rebuking Peter in front of the others saying,

> *...Get thee behind me, Satan: for thou savourest not the*
> *things that be of God, but the things that be of men. And*
> *when he had called the people unto him with his disci-*
> *ples also, he said unto them, Whosoever will come after*
> *me, let him deny himself, and take up his cross, and fol-*
> *low me. For whosoever will save his life shall lose it; but*
> *whosoever shall lose his life for my sake and the gos-*
> *pel's, the same shall save it. For what shall it profit a*
> *man, if he shall gain the whole world, and lose his own*
> *soul? Or what shall a man give in exchange for his soul?*
> *Whosoever therefore shall be ashamed of me and of my*
> *words in this adulterous and sinful generation; of him*
> *also shall the Son of man be ashamed, when he cometh*
> *in the glory of his Father with the holy angels.*

Mark 8:33-38

This confrontation between Jesus and Peter shows the mentality of
the Jewish people and their *deeply* held beliefs of what their Savior
was expected to do. They believed when their Savior or in the Hebrew language, *Messiah,* arrived on the scene He would rescue them
from their Roman oppressors. So when Jesus spoke about dying on
a cross it confused not only Peter, but the majority of the Israelite
people. Jesus had every intention of being their Savior, just not in
the time frame they had presupposed. When the Jews studied the
Old Testament Scriptures they believed when their Messiah came
He would arrive to defeat their enemies because of Scriptures like
this one from *Isaiah:*

> *...his name shall be called Wonderful, Counsellor, The*
> *mighty God, The everlasting Father, The Prince of*
> *Peace. Of the increase of his government and peace there*
> *shall be no end, upon the throne of David, and upon his*
> *kingdom, to order it, and to establish it with judgment*
> *and with justice from henceforth even for ever.*

Isaiah 9:6-7

The Jews had read in the Old Testament scriptures that their Savior would come to them in power and might, believing He would deliver them from their enemies just as God had done for them in days past when the Egyptians had enslaved them. Unfortunately, they misunderstood their Messiah was going to come twice! During His first appearance He would be clothed in humility and His purpose would be to bear the sins of the world, providing redemption for those who would put their trust in Him. After completing this mission of providing reconciliation to men through His shed blood on the cross, at the perfect time, then and only then, would He come again and destroy Israel's enemies, rescuing them *and all who call upon His name for eternal salvation!*

Thirdly, Jesus prophesied about the end of the world and His 2nd coming. *Matthew* 24 is a great chapter to study on this subject. In this chapter the disciples asked Jesus privately, *"...what shall be the sign of thy coming, and of the end of the world" (Mt 24:3)?* Jesus provided many details about the end, and one of the major signs is highlighted in the following excerpt from this exciting, yet, dreadful chapter:

> *...they deliver you up to be afflicted, and shall kill you: and ye shall be hated of all nations for my name's sake. And then shall many be offended, and shall betray one another, and shall hate one another. And many false prophets shall rise, and shall deceive many. And because iniquity [sin] shall abound, the love of many shall wax cold. But he that shall endure unto the end, the same shall be saved. And this gospel of the kingdom shall be preached in all the world for a witness unto all nations; and then shall the end come.*

> *Matthew 24:9-14*

Jesus made it clear His followers will be persecuted in the end times. As well, He prophesied many false prophets will utter lies which deceive masses of people. Also during the end times, sin will consume cultures around the world. Lastly, in this passage, Jesus affirmed the Gospel will be preached in all nations just before the end. Later in Matthew 24 Jesus explains that at the end He will return to judge the wicked and bring His children, those who have trusted in Him, home to His Heavenly Kingdom. Jesus spoke of His 2nd coming by saying,

> And then shall appear the sign of the Son of man in heaven: and then shall all the tribes of the earth mourn, and they shall see the Son of man coming in the clouds of heaven with power and great glory. And he shall send his angels with a great sound of a trumpet, and they shall gather together his elect from the four winds, from one end of heaven to the other.

Matthew 24:30-31

Interestingly, in this passage Jesus is referencing Daniel's prophecy as He prophecies about His 2nd coming (Dn 7). The second coming of Christ is a powerful event in God's story every Christian is eagerly awaiting. Understandably, Jesus' disciples hoped while He was on the earth during their lives, He would bring His story to a close, but that was not His perfect plan. No, in fact, God's story was only taking a new twist and they were to be main characters in His plot line! Jesus' 2nd coming is so important that it is the sixth section of *The Gospel Octagon*. But first, Jesus had a monumental mission, to die for the sins of humanity on a cross and rise from the grave to defeat the curse which Adam and Eve had brought upon the whole world when they rebelled against their Creator in the Garden of Eden.

Jesus' Death & Resurrection

God's divine storyline is now reaching its pinnacle! The life of Jesus Christ is the climax of God's story for mankind. What becomes even more gripping is the realization that the *climax* of the climax is Jesus Christ's death and resurrection. **God's story now**

**begins tightening up as prophecy and purpose entwine,
creating the most epic moments history can ever boast of.**
God sent Himself, wrapped in flesh, to the earth He created. He experienced all the temptations and trials a man could face, for one
ultimate purpose: to redeem mankind's soul and buy it back from
the consequence the slave of sin is doomed to face. Man became a
slave to sin back in the Garden of Eden. When Adam and Eve sinned
against God there was an immediate separation between God and
man. God's eternal, perfect laws required the separation. That is,
God could not have fellowship with a being who rejected full obedience to Him. Therefore, once sin entered the world through Adam
and Eve's rebellion their relationship with God was profoundly sev-
ered. Yet, God is the Author of the story. He knew their rebellion
would occur. So He allowed them to rebel, because He knew His
story's ending would glorify Himself and offer redemption to those
He created in His image (Gn 1:27). **The only possible way the
story could end to save humanity and glorify God would be
for God Himself to become a man, live a sinless life, die for
the sins of man, and then rise from the grave defeating the
curse of sin.** The reason this was the only way is because God's law
declares this to be so. If God is perfect, then His laws are perfect.
God's laws are perfect. Therefore, God is perfect and all of His
Words and His plans for humanity are perfect.

**The time was at hand for the blood of the spotless
Lamb of God to wash away the sins of the world!** Jesus had
healed the broken, taught truth, and raised up disciples to continue
spreading the truth after He was gone. The only thing left to accomplish was His main reason for coming into the world: To go to the
cross bearing the sins of the world, and rise from the dead to break
the curse of sin which separated man from having a pure relationship with God.

Throughout Jesus' earthly ministry the religious leaders in power hated Him. Jesus continually rebuked them and their teachings, often calling them hypocrites. He even publicly declared them to be a brood of vipers, which is not a compliment in any culture! The religious leaders thought Jesus was a fraud. Only, *they* were the real frauds. They did not recognize the One they had preached about, even when He was talking to them face to face. As Jesus had said, they were indeed hypocrites! After three to three and a half years of Jesus' ministry, the religious leaders in power moved into action. Jesus was becoming more and more popular with the people as time went by and many of His followers thought He was going to save them from their oppressors. The religious leaders felt their own power being threatened. Because they feared Jesus' followers, the decision was made to arrest Him in secret (Mt 26:4). Unexpectedly, as one reads through the first four books of the New Testament the reader discovers one of Jesus' 12 disciples played the traitor. Jesus was aware of the traitor, but He used Him, as He does all the wicked, for His purposes and His glory. Jesus prophesied about Judas, the betrayer (Mt 26:21). This man was a money-hungry lover of himself, not the things of God. Jesus knew of Judas' evil ways, but He picked him to be His disciple, because **God uses those who reject Him to teach Truth.** He is the Author. He has the pen and uses the free choices of people to write His script. God did not force Judas to reject Him. Judas acted and God used Judas' free will in His divine storyline. Judas was the one who agreed, for a price of 30 silver pieces, to find out for the religious leaders where and when Jesus would be alone in the night hours so they could arrest Him in darkness. One unforgettable night the priests did arrest Jesus and brought Him before the high council of religious leaders to be questioned.

During their interrogation the High Priest asked Jesus, *"...I adjure thee by the living God, that thou tell us whether thou be the Christ,*

the Son of God" (Mt 26:63). For the previous questions Jesus had remained silent, but when the High Priest demanded an answer of
Him for this question Jesus responded by saying, *"...Thou hast said:
nevertheless I say unto you, Hereafter shall ye see the Son of man sitting
on the right hand of power, and coming in the clouds of heaven" (Mt
26:64).* Jesus' words brought anger to the High priest, so much so he
*"...rent his clothes, saying, He hath spoken blasphemy; what further need
have we of witnesses? behold, now ye have heard his blasphemy" (Mt
26:65).* The High Priest ripped his clothes, which was a common
thing for Israelites to do when expressing their inward feelings out-
wardly. He accused Jesus' words of blaspheming God. Now if Jesus
was not truly God in the flesh this would be true, but **they truly
did have the Creator of Life on trial.** Then, the High Priest
turned to his fellow leaders and the judgement of death was cast.
Next, *"...they spit in his face, and buffeted [hit] him; and others smote him
with the palms of their hands, Saying, Prophesy unto us, thou Christ, Who
is he that smote thee" (Mt 26:66-68)?*

    After Jesus' own people rejected Him, they used the local
political leaders, Pilate and Herod, to legally execute the judgement.
Neither Pilate nor Herod believed Jesus deserved death, but the Israelites put political pressure on Pilate. Pilate tried to avoid murder-
ing Jesus by first having His body severely scourged. All his at-
tempts to persuade the Jewish leadership to let Jesus go free failed.
Fearful of an uprising, Pilate issued the execution of Jesus of Nazareth (Mt 27:24). Jesus was officially sentenced to death by the Roman government through crucifixion. "Crucifixion was universally
recognized as the most horrible type of death."[75] After His body was
scourged and the mock trial was over, Jesus carried His own cross to
the place where He would finish out His agonizing and bloody sentence for the sins of the world. Once they reached the mountain of
Golgotha, the executioners drove nails into Jesus' body, hanging

Him upon His cross which was then raised up so all could view Him in His torturing pain until He died (Mt 27; Mk 15; Lk 23; Jn 19).

Although Jesus was sentenced to death, the Bible reveals He did not die by crucifixion, rather, He *"...yielded up the ghost" (Mt 27:50).* As soon as Jesus' Spirit left His body, the Bible tells us four amazing things happened. First, the veil of the temple was torn in two. (The temple Solomon had built was where the Spirit of God resided to commune with the priests.) This veil separated the rest of the temple from the Holy of Holies where God's mercy seat was located on which the blood of lambs was poured for covering of sins. Only the Levitical priests were allowed to enter after much cleansing and bearing sacrificial blood. The tearing of this veil symbolized that God had entered His own temple with His own sacrificial blood and no longer was the blood of lambs needed. God's Spirit was accessible to all men and the price of sin had been paid once and for all. Second, a great earthquake shook the land. Third, many faithful people of God were raised from the dead. Fourth, The Bible reports that some of Jesus' Roman murderers came to believe Jesus was God. The record of this is in *Matthew 27:54*, which says, *"Now when the centurion, and they that were with him, watching Jesus, saw the earthquake, and those things that were done, they feared greatly, saying, Truly this was the Son of God."*

As it came time to bury Jesus, Pilate gave the body to one of Jesus' followers, Joseph of Arimathea, who had requested it. Joseph placed Jesus in his own personal tomb, which was in a cut out rock. On the following day, the religious leaders, who had demanded the death sentence, encouraged Pilate to place a watch of guards around Jesus' tomb since He had prophesied He would rise from the dead after three days. The religious leaders were afraid Jesus' disciples would come by night and steal the body, claiming He had risen.

They wished to put to silence Jesus' name and memory forever and prove this "alleged" Messiah a fraud.

> *Now the next day, that followed the day of the prepara-*
> *tion, the chief priests and Pharisees came together unto*
> *Pilate, Saying, Sir, we remember that that deceiver said,*
> *while he was yet alive, After three days I will rise*
> *again. Command therefore that the sepulchre [tomb] be*
> *made sure [secure] until the third day, lest his disciples*
> *come by night, and steal him away, and say unto the*
> *people, He is risen from the dead: so the last error shall*
> *be worse than the first. Pilate said unto them, Ye have a*
> *watch: go your way, make it as sure as ye can. So they*
> *went, and made the sepulchre sure, sealing the stone, and*
> *setting a watch.*

Matthew 27:62-66

As He had prophesied, three days after being crucified Jesus rose from the dead! The scene unfolded in an incredible fashion! Beginning early in the morning of the third day there was an earthquake as two angels appeared on the scene. When the guards on watch saw the angel(s) they shook with fear and fainted (Mt 28:4). The angels rolled the great stone covering the mouth of the tomb away from the entrance. It should be noted that Jesus did not need help opening the door to let Him out, rather they rolled the stone away to allow the miracle to be seen by His disciples, because some of them were on their way to anoint Him with burial spices, as was customary for their dead. Upon arriving, the disciples encountered the angels and these heavenly beings informed them Jesus had risen from the dead as He had said He would. They told the disciples to go tell the others about His resurrection from the dead, and He would meet them in Galilee (Mk 16:6-7). They rushed back to tell everyone, but no one would believe them. Peter and John however, immediately took off running to the place where Jesus had been laid to see if their friend's testimony bore truth. Peter arrived first and found the tomb empty with Jesus' burial wrappings inside (Lk 24:12). His Lord was not there. He feared Jesus' body had been stolen! John finally caught up and too saw the grave clothes his Lord had left behind, but he believed Jesus had been raised! **Jesus had indeed risen, conquering death and fulfilling His plan for the redemption of men!** His blood had been shed, His mission had been accomplished! He had died to win the prize! **The reward He gained was the legal right to break the curse of man's sin for those who loved Him so one day they could be with Him forever, cleansed and purified in His blood, which washes away all sin!**

The morning Jesus arose He appeared first to Mary and then to all of the women disciples who had traveled with her to the grave. Next, He appeared to two of His followers traveling from Jerusalem to Emmaus, a seven mile journey (Lk 24:13-34). Later that night He appeared to His chosen disciples. The sight of Jesus brought fear, for most had not believed their companion's testimonies! They couldn't believe their eyes, for they thought He was a spirit (Lk 24:37). Jesus calmed their fears as He spoke to them, showing them the scars in His hands and feet as proof He had indeed risen from the dead! The disciples were astonished (Lk 24:41)! That night He opened the Scriptures and said,

...These are the words which I spake [spoke] unto you, while I was yet with you, that all things must be fulfilled, which were written in the law of Moses, and in the prophets, and in the psalms, concerning me. Then opened he their understanding, that they might understand the scriptures, And said unto them, Thus it is written, and thus it behooved Christ to suffer, and to rise from the dead the third day: And that repentance and remission of sins should be preached in his name among all nations, beginning at Jerusalem. And ye are witnesses of these things. And, behold, I send the promise of my Father upon you: but tarry ye in the city of Jerusalem, until ye be endued with power from on high.

Luke 24:44-53

All together, Jesus remained on the earth 40 days in His resurrected body, teaching His disciples (Ac 1:3). Then, at His appointed time He returned to His Heavenly Kingdom. Before He ascended into the clouds Jesus gave His disciples one last word. He said,

> ...*All power is given unto me in heaven and in earth. Go ye therefore, and teach all nations, baptizing them in the name of the Father, and of the Son, and of the Holy Ghost [Spirit]: Teaching them to observe all things whatsoever I have commanded you: and, lo, I am with you always, even unto the end of the world. Amen.*
>
> *Matthew 28:16-20*

As Jesus ascended into the sky the disciples locked their eyes on Him. Suddenly, two angels appeared in their midst and said, "...*Ye men of Galilee, why stand ye gazing up into heaven? this same Jesus, which is taken up from you into heaven, shall so come in like manner as ye have seen him go into heaven*" *(Ac 1:11)*. As the disciples journeyed home, the Bible says they "*returned to Jerusalem with great joy*" *(Lk 24:52)*.

Chapter Five

THE CHURCH

"And suddenly there came a sound from heaven as of a rushing mighty wind, and it filled all the house where they were sitting. And there appeared unto them cloven tongues like as of fire, and it sat upon each of them. And they were all filled with the Holy Ghost [Spirit], and began to speak with other tounges [languages], as the Spirit gave them utterance."

Acts 2:2-4

The Story Line

After the climax of the death and resurrection of Jesus Christ, God created the church to proclaim His Gospel message of light and truth in a world of darkness and lies. The church began 2,000 years ago on God's story line, but we are still at this part in the plot today. The church includes Jewish and Gentile (non Jewish) believers in Christ. For Jewish believers in God, the church is a continuation of their faith under God's new covenant. For Gentile believers in God, their faith is grafted into the branch of the Israelites, for they are the people whom God created for Himself.

The Church Begins

Once Jesus arose from the dead, He told His disciples that after He ascended into heaven He would send the Holy Spirit to teach and guide them throughout their lives. The disciples waited in Jerusalem together patiently. Then, on the Jewish holiday of Pentecost, which is 50 days after Passover, the Holy Spirit descended upon the disciples and they all began speaking in different languages! The people in town were astonished, for the disciples (who were only common people) were speaking languages they had no way of knowing. At this time in Jerusalem there were Jews from every nation who had come to celebrate Pentecost, many of whom spoke different languages. As they heard the disciples speaking in their own native tongues and were able to understand them, they began asking, *"What meaneth this" (Ac 2:12)?* Using their question, Peter capitalized on the opportunity and preached the first sermon of the church, which is recorded in *Acts* 2. He got straight to the point by saying,

> *...Ye men of Israel, hear these words; Jesus of Nazareth, a man approved of God among you by miracles and wonders and signs, which God did by him in the midst of you, as ye yourselves also know: Him, being delivered by the determinate counsel and foreknowledge of God, ye have taken, and by wicked hands have crucified and slain: Whom God hath raised up, having loosed the pains of death: because it was not possible that he should be holden of it.*

Acts 2:22-24

Peter is plainly testifying the Jews knew full well Jesus had been sent from God! They were given ample proof in all the powerful miracles He had performed, yet they chose to slay the Son of God regardless. God knew this would happen though, and Jesus had risen from the dead to fulfill the words of the prophets. Later in his sermon, Peter explained the disciples were able to speak in various languages because the Holy Spirit enabled them to (Ac 2:32-33).

The Holy Spirit is referred to throughout the Scriptures as the Helper and the Counselor. How true this is for it wasn't until the disciples received God's Spirit that they went into the streets to preach about Christ. Since that wonderful day, **God's true disciples have been faithful in proclaiming the Gospel!** As Peter drew near the end of his message, he concluded with, *"Therefore let all the house of Israel know assuredly, that God hath made the same Jesus, whom ye have crucified, both Lord and Christ" (Ac 2:36).* After Peter's sermon the Scriptures record 3,000 people felt the conviction of God and they asked the disciples, *"what shall we do" (Ac 2:37)!?* Peter answered them saying,

> *Repent, and be baptized every one of you in the name of Jesus Christ for the remission of sins, and ye shall receive the gift of the Holy Ghost [Spirit]. For the promise is unto you, and to your children, and to all that are afar off, even as many as the Lord our God shall call. And with many other words did he testify and exhort, saying, Save yourselves from this untoward [wicked] generation.*

Acts 2:36-40

The Holy Spirit came to the disciples 10 days after Jesus ascended into heaven, on the day of Pentecost. Pentecost was a Jewish holiday commemorating when the Israelites received God's law on Mount Sinai.[76] The law did two primary things: One, it revealed sin. Two, it taught the Israelites how to live for God. Likewise, **The Holy Spirit's purpose is to convict one of sin and teach God's children how to live for God.** The law does not save, only Jesus saves. Yet, the law has a purpose! **The law leads a person to understand his or her need for Jesus, the only Savior, by exposing their sin.** Then, once he or she believes in Christ, The Holy Spirit dwells inside of them and guides them to live for God.

That day of Pentecost generated the birth of the church into the world! *Acts 1:15* tells us after Jesus' earthly ministry, there were

only 120 believers who gathered together. By modern church stan-
dards, that would not be considered successful. However, God never
has measured success by numbers. God's definition of success is
when one has a humble heart and follows after His words of truth in
obedience. God is able to greatly use those who obey Him with a
pure heart. When Peter preached his first sermon 3,000 people
chose to follow Christ! That is amazing, but it is important to remember that large numbers should never be the focus of Jesus' disciples. The focus should always be proclaiming God's Word truthfully, whether it changes one life or millions.

God uses His church to shine His light in an exceedingly
dark world. Prior to the church, Israel was set apart to live for God.
**Both Israel and the church were created by God to be a
light to the world, but in different ways.** Israel was called to
be a light through obeying and teaching the laws of Moses. The
church was called to be a light through obeying God's Word and
spreading the Gospel. Evil leaders arose in Israel and also arise in
the church leading many to reject the mission God gave them (Jd 4).
This is no surprise to God. He is the Author and His story has unfolded as He foreknew from the beginning!

Just as Jesus' healing ministry drew crowds to His preaching, so God enabled His disciples to heal, displaying to everyone
these men were following in their Master's footsteps.

Miraculous Healing

The Holy Spirit enabled Jesus' disciples to heal the broken.
One such example happened soon after the church was birthed. The
Bible records a lame man who was healed by Peter and John. The
man had been crippled since birth, so each day he laid near the temple gate to beg for money. As Peter and John were walking, the lame
man asked them for money. Peter responded with words the man

had never heard before. Peter said, *"Silver and gold have I none; but such as I have give I thee: In the name of Jesus Christ of Nazareth rise up and walk" (Ac 3:7).* Amazingly, the man got up and walked! The Scriptures record the man, *"...leaping up stood, and walked, and entered with them into the temple, walking, and leaping, and praising God" (Ac 3:8).* When those standing nearby witnessed the lame man's healing and saw him walking and praising God, they were dumbfounded. When Peter observed the response of the gathering crowd he followed Jesus' example and began preaching the truth saying,

> *...Ye men of Israel, why marvel ye at this? or why look ye so earnestly on us, as though by our own power or holiness we had made this man to walk? The God of Abraham, and of Isaac, and of Jacob, the God of our fathers, hath glorified his Son Jesus; whom ye delivered up, and denied him in the presence of Pilate, when he was determined to let him go. But ye denied the Holy One and the Just, and desired a murderer to be granted unto you; And killed the Prince of life, whom God hath raised from the dead; whereof we are witnesses. And his name through faith in his name hath made this man strong, whom ye see and know: yea, the faith which is by him hath given him this perfect soundness in the presence of you all. And now, brethren, I wot that through ignorance ye did it, as did also your rulers. But those things, which God before had shewed [showed] by the mouth of all his prophets, that Christ should suffer, he hath so fulfilled. Repent ye therefore, and be converted, that your sins may be blotted out, when the times of refreshing shall come from the presence of the Lord. And he shall send Jesus Christ, which before was preached unto you: Whom the heaven must receive until the times of restitution of all things, which God hath spoken by the mouth of all his holy prophets since the world began. For Moses truly said unto the fathers, A prophet shall the Lord your God raise up unto you of your brethren, like unto me; him shall ye hear in all things whatsoever he shall say unto you. And it shall come to pass, that every soul, which will not hear that prophet, shall be destroyed from among the people. Yea, and all the prophets from Samuel and those that follow after, as many as have spoken, have likewise foretold of these days. Ye are the children of the prophets,*

and of the covenant which God made with our fathers,
saying unto Abraham, And in thy seed shall all the kin-
dreds of the earth be blessed. Unto you first God, having
raised up his Son Jesus, sent him to bless you, in turning
away every one of you from his iniquities.

Acts 3:12-26

The Holy Spirit had worked through Peter to heal and to speak these words to the crowd. The Spirit led Peter to explain how all of the Israelite's history tied into what they'd just witnessed with their very eyes. **The crippled man's faith in Jesus healed him!** The man probably held very low thoughts about himself, but God had a purpose for His life, just as He does for every person!

As the church grew The Holy Spirit continued empowering the disciples to accomplish great and mighty deeds which always glorified God. Yet, just as Jesus was persecuted for His teachings, so also His disciples were and still are persecuted.

Persecution

Persecution of the church began immediately after the church was born. In fact, Peter and John were arrested when they healed the lame man because they were preaching Jesus had been raised from the dead (Ac 4). Following the day of their arrest the religious leaders gathered together to question the two disciples. They asked, *"By what power, or by what name, have ye done this" (Ac 4:7)?* Peter responded by saying,

...Ye rulers of the people, and elders of Israel, If we this
day be examined of the good deed done to the impotent
man, by what means he is made whole; Be it known unto
you all, and to all the people of Israel, that by the name
of Jesus Christ of Nazareth, whom ye crucified, whom
God raised from the dead, even by him doth this man
stand here before you whole. This is the stone which was
set at nought of you builders, which is become the head
of the corner. Neither is there salvation in any other: for

there is none other name under heaven given among
men, whereby we must be saved.

Acts 4:8-12

The council of leaders found themselves in a difficult position. They didn't believe Peter's words, but they couldn't deny the miracle which the people had witnessed, for many knew of this cripple and had seen the true healing. So the council decided to threaten these men, warning them to no longer teach about Jesus. They didn't know how else to punish them for the great crowd testified of the incredible healing.

This episode was one of the first examples of persecution the church faced, but as time went on, persecution intensified rapidly. The threat of jail time didn't frighten the disciples. Quite the contrary, they continued to preach the Gospel fearlessly, and many flocked to them for healing in Jesus' name. Their popularity among the people ignited great jealousy amongst the religious leaders. Soon Peter and John were thrown in jail for the second time. But this time God sent an angel to set them free and the angel instructed the disciples, *"Go, stand and speak in the temple to the people all the words of this life" (Ac 5:20).* They were faithful in obeying! The next day the council gathered together to meet with the imprisoned disciples only to discover they were missing from their prison quarters! Upon hearing that Jesus' disciples were teaching in the temple, the council demanded Peter and John be arrested immediately. After further questioning and conversing with the council members, the disciples were flogged (severely beaten), and told never again to teach about Jesus. The council then set them free.

Shortly after their flogging, persecution against the church grew far worse. In *Acts* 6-7 the Bible records the story of Stephen, the disciple. The Bible tells us Stephen was a faithful man whom

God had used to display His power. Viciously, some evil men lied about him saying he had blasphemed both Moses' and God's name. Stephen was arrested and questioned. When the council interrogated Stephen he told them the truth of what he believed. He began with Abraham and explained everything up until the present time. The people were in full agreement with his lengthly account of what he believed... until he said these words,

> *Ye stiffnecked and uncircumcised in heart and ears, ye do always resist the Holy Ghost [Spirit]: as your fathers did, so do ye. Which of the prophets have not your fathers persecuted? and they have slain them which shewed [showed] before of the coming of the Just One; of whom ye have been now the betrayers and murderers: Who have received the law by the disposition of angels, and have not kept it.*

> *Acts 7:51-53*

Stephen's declaration enraged the council. As he viewed their evil, anger filled faces, God appeared to him and he saw *"...the glory of God, and Jesus standing on the right hand of God" (Ac 7:55)*. When Stephen declared his vision to the council the Scriptures say, *"...they cried out with a loud voice, and stopped their ears, and ran upon him with one accord, And cast him out of the city, and stoned him: and the witnesses laid down their clothes at a young man's feet, whose name was Saul" (Ac 7:57-58)*. As the stones began to hit Stephen one by one he began *"...calling upon God, and saying, Lord Jesus, receive my spirit. And he kneeled down, and cried with a loud voice, Lord, lay not this sin to their charge. And when he had said this, he fell asleep" (Ac 7:59-60)*. Stephen was truly a godly man faithful to His Creator, Savior, and Lord to the end of his earthly life. After Stephen's murder,

> *...there was a great persecution against the church which was at Jerusalem; and they were all scattered abroad throughout the regions of Judaea and Samaria, except the apostles. And devout men carried Stephen to his burial, and made great lamentation over him. As for Saul, he*

made havock of the church, entering into every house,
and haling men and women committed them to prison.

Acts 8:1-3

From this time forward, the persecution of the church goes wild, especially in Jerusalem. The persecutors' intent was to crush the spread of the Gospel. Instead, it lit a blazing fire under the early church which furthered the preaching of the Gospel! This persecution caused God's faithful to flee, taking the message of truth with them to other parts of the world and setting aflame many more hearts to honor and follow Christ. Saul, one of the younger religious leaders, the one who approved of Stephen's murder, became a forceful leader in persecuting the church. But Saul soon encountered the light of God and his life was forever changed.

While Saul was traveling to Damascus with the intent to destroy Jesus' disciples, the glorified Christ confronted him. Jesus was arrayed in blinding brightness which caused Saul to fall off his horse and onto the dirt path. As Saul was laying in the dust God spoke to him saying, *"...Saul, Saul, why persecutest thou me? And he said, Who art thou, Lord? And the Lord said, I am Jesus whom thou persecutest: ...And he trembling and astonished said, Lord, what wilt thou have me to do" (Ac 9:3-6)?* God instructed Saul to continue on to Damascus and await His further instruction. When Saul got up from the ground he discovered he was blind! His emotions must have been racing, for not only had he heard God speaking to him, but had learned he was dreadfully wrong and Jesus truly is the God of his fathers! Once Saul arrived in Damascus The Lord led Ananias, a faithful believer, to pray for Saul so he may receive his sight back and be filled with The Holy Spirit. Once Ananias prayed the Scriptures record, *"...immediately there fell from his eyes as it had been scales: and he received sight forthwith, and arose, and was baptized" (Ac 9:18).* Just as the New Testament teaches, when someone puts their faith in Jesus for the forgiveness of their sins, they get baptized. **Baptism does not save, only Jesus saves, but baptism is a public profession of the inward reality that one has been born again.** After regaining his strength, Saul stayed with the Damascus disciples a few days, undoubtedly to learn more about Jesus' teachings from those who knew Him personally. Then, Saul began entering the synagogues (Jewish places of worship) where he preached Jesus was truly their long awaited Messiah, *"the Son of God" (Ac 9:20)*. His preaching was so convincing the Jews were unable to provide a logical answer to why he was wrong (Ac 9:22). Due to his constant and powerful preaching he became a target of persecution. It wasn't long before there was a death sentence on his head, but God spared him, for the Lord had special plans for Saul's life. As time passed, God gave Saul a new name to go with his new life in Christ; Saul's new name was Paul.

Paul became a primary instrument God used to share His Gospel throughout the world. God used Paul to plant churches. He traveled from one city to another and when he found faithful believers he taught them everything he could and helped them build a church for a short season. Then he would leave the church in the hands of local leaders and move on to the next city where he'd start the whole process over again. Throughout his life Paul endured much persecution, yet, his faith in God remained strong to the end. Paul not only planted churches, but God also used him to write two thirds of the New Testament Scriptures. He brought so much agitation towards those who were enemies of the Christian faith that he was executed for his beliefs. Not only did Paul die a martyr, but many disciples were also persecuted to the point of death for their testimony about Jesus Christ.[77]

Persecution was not something unexpected in the lives of the disciples, for Jesus Himself warned His disciples they would be persecuted (Jn 15:20). Persecution of Jesus' disciples did (and still does) happen for multiple reasons. Sometimes persecution came from Jewish believers like Saul, who did not believe Jesus was the Messiah. Other times persecution came about because of secular, political reasons. Ironically, persecution (usually non-physical) sometimes came from within the church through false prophets and teachers. Jesus even warned His disciples how false teaching could infect a healthy church just like a virus infects a healthy person (Mt 7:15; 16:6; 24:4-5; 24).

False Prophets/Teachers
God warned the Israelites about false prophets. He also warned His disciples about them (Mt 24:24). Remember, a false *prophet* is someone claiming to speak for God, when in actuality God never spoke to them. Thus, they are deceivers. Whereas, a false *teacher* is someone who intentionally teaches God's Word incorrectly to deceive people from following the truth. Jesus went as far to say *"...there shall arise false Christs, and false prophets, and shall shew [show] great signs and wonders; insomuch that, if it were possible, they shall deceive the very elect" (Mt 24:24).* Jesus' words were a warning to the disciples then and to us today. Staggeringly, He said false prophets would affirm their words by performing miracles! The deception will be so cunningly hypnotic many people who claim to follow Jesus will be deceived. Jesus' words highlight that there are numerous people who claim to be His followers, but they truly are not (Mt 7:22-23). Those who will be deceived reject God's Word, and choose to follow the false prophets and teachers who claim to speak from God, but do not: they are only liars.

Jesus also said *"Woe unto you, when all men shall speak well of you! for so did their fathers to the false prophets" (Lk 6:26).* Although this may sound unusual, many people love false prophets, except of course, God and His true children. Peter wrote about false prophets in detail in *2 Peter*. He explained that just as there were false prophets in days gone by, there will also be the same kind of people amongst the church, *"who privily shall bring in damnable heresies, even denying the Lord that bought them, and bring upon themselves swift destruction" (2 Pt 2:1)*. Jude, the half brother of Jesus, wrote his New Testament letter specifically to expose people of this very nature. His writing focused on exposing how false teachers are in the midst of the church body teaching God's grace gives people the freedom to live a sinful lifestyle, and thereby *"denying the only Lord God, and our Lord Jesus Christ" (Jd 4)*. He goes on to describe these type of people in great detail saying they *"...are murmurers, [and] complainers, walking after their own lusts; and their mouth speaketh great swelling words, having men's persons in admiration because of advantage [for their own gain]" (Jd 16)*. Jude continues on even further, using an allegory to describe these false teachers. He said,

> *Woe unto them! for they have gone in the way of Cain... These are spots in your feasts of charity, when they feast with you, feeding themselves without fear: clouds they are without water, carried about of winds; trees whose fruit withereth, without fruit, twice dead, plucked up by the roots; Raging waves of the sea, foaming out their own shame; wandering stars, to whom is reserved the blackness of darkness for ever.*

Jude 11-13

During the early church there were many false prophets and teachers. Jesus prophesied about them. Peter, John, Paul and Jude warned about these liars, too. They not only warned the believers of their day, but also the ones to come (2 Pt 2:1; 1 Jn 4:1; 1 Tm 4:1-3; Jd 4). The apostles warned believers because God's Kingdom is a Kingdom of Truth and God's Word can not be altered. When we know the truth, we are set free from the lies of this world and can begin living the kingdom lifestyle here on the earth, glorifying our Father in heaven (Jn 8:32).

Kingdom Lifestyle

The Kingdom of God has been the hope of God's children since sin entered the world in the Garden of Eden. **Entrance into God's Kingdom is the future event for every born-again believer in Jesus Christ (Jn 3:3).** Until that glorious day arrives, Jesus gave His disciples clarity on how to live for Him in this fallen world.

One day during Jesus' earthly ministry, a scribe (someone employed for his ability to read and write)[78] asked Him a question, *"What is the first [greatest] commandment of all" (Mk 12:28)?* Jesus responded by saying,

> *The first of all the commandments is, Hear, O Israel; The Lord our God is one Lord: And thou shalt love the Lord thy God with all thy heart, and with all thy soul, and with all thy mind, and with all thy strength: this is the first commandment.*
>
> *Mark 12:29-30*

Even on this side of God's Kingdom His children are called to love God with all of their heart, soul, mind, and strength. Yes, people fall short because of sin, but when sin is recognized in our life we must quickly repent, get back up, and pursue living for God perfectly (Mt 5:48). When a person puts their faith in Jesus and trusts in Him as the Lord of their life they are born-again (Jn 3:7). **God sees every born again believer as perfect in His eyes because of the blood of Christ.** Yet, in our human nature we are not perfect because we still fall into sin. We can have confidence in knowing we are right with God because of Jesus' sacrifice, yet, we must still strive to live for God perfectly, not because we are earning our salvation, for salvation is a free gift, but because our pursuit of living for God perfectly is proof we are seeking to obey Him with all of our heart, soul, mind and strength. We are saved by faith but our actions display our faith is genuine. Living out the greatest commandment is how God calls His children to live in this world. **When we pursue loving God in a whole hearted way we are truly living out the kingdom lifestyle, even before we enter through the pearly gates to the eternal Kingdom of God!**

The Mission

On the day of Pentecost, when the Holy Spirit filled the believers, God's church was born. The Lord had a purpose and mission for His church summed up in Jesus' last words to His disciples. *"Go ye therefore, and teach all nations, baptizing them in the name of the Father, and of the Son, and of the Holy Ghost [Spirit]: Teaching them to observe all things whatsoever I have commanded you..." (Mt 28:19-20).* This command was given to the disciples of then and all those to follow, that they should teach everyone the truth of the Scriptures.

The disciples were obedient to Jesus, which is why the church still exists today. The Lord equipped the disciples to work miracles by His Spirit for the purpose of bringing glory to His name. **When Christ's followers were persecuted, they rejoiced because they knew this world was not their home; they had hope in Jesus' return and God's eternal kingdom.** Their faith was genuine and built upon the solid rock of Truth. The disciples spent their lives in spreading the Gospel because they knew their God was alive! Jesus had become a most precious, intimate friend and they were more than willing to die for their Creator and Savior. **Jesus commanded His Church to share the Gospel until He returned, for He promised to come again to trample His enemies and welcome His children into His heavenly kingdom!**

The End Times Tribulation

The end times is a phrase speaking about the last years of the human age, just before the return of Jesus to earth. The early church spent time teaching about the end times because Jesus had. In fact, the book of *Revelation* focuses much of its contents on this frightening and exciting time of God's story. *Revelation* is the last book in the Bible, written by the apostle, John. God gave John a glorious revelation about amazing future events which will bring to a close the later part of His story. The book begins with Jesus saying, *"Blessed is he that readeth, and they that hear the words of this prophecy, and keep those things which are written therein: for the time is at hand" (Rv 1:3).* The Writer of the beginning and end of all things tells us that those who read this book will be blessed. I strongly encourage you to read the book of *Revelation*. While Jesus walked the earth He gave a detailed description about this time period in *Matthew 24*. The prophets, Daniel and Joel, also wrote heavily about the end times. There are many details and signs to study and watch for, which the prophets, Jesus, and the apostles taught and unveiled. Let's look at some of the major signs together.

The Scriptures reveal the end times will last for seven years, and there will be signs signifying the beginning-of-the-end is near prior to that seven year period (Dn 9). Some of these signs are: liars claiming to be Jesus, wars, threats of wars, famine, disease, and numerous earthquakes (Mt 24:4-8).

Regarding the last seven years of earth history there will be many more signs confirming The King is saddling up to enter center stage! Three of the major signs Jesus unveiled are: increased persecution of Christians, the Gospel being preached to every people group in the world, and unusual signs in the heavens (Mt 24:9-14; 29). A few more of the major signs are revealed by Paul in his letter to the church at Thessolanica, in which he wrote,

> *Now we beseech you, brethren, by the coming of our Lord Jesus Christ, and by our gathering together unto him, That ye be not soon shaken in mind, or be troubled,*

*neither by spirit, nor by word, nor by letter as from us, as
that the day of Christ is at hand. Let no man deceive you
by any means: for that day shall not come, except there
come a falling away first, and that man of sin be revealed, the son of perdition; Who opposeth and exalteth
himself above all that is called God, or that is worshipped; so that he as God sitteth in the temple of God,
shewing [showing] himself that he is God. Remember ye
not, that, when I was yet with you, I told you these
things? And now ye know what withholdeth that he might
be revealed in his time. For the mystery of iniquity doth
already work: only he who now letteth will let, until he
be taken out of the way. And then shall that Wicked be
revealed, whom the Lord shall consume with the spirit of
his mouth, and shall destroy with the brightness of his
coming: Even him, whose coming is after the working of
Satan with all power and signs and lying wonders, And
with all deceivableness of unrighteousness in them that
perish; because they received not the love of the truth,
that they might be saved. And for this cause God shall
send them strong delusion, that they should believe a
lie: That they all might be damned who believed not the
truth, but had pleasure in unrighteousness.*

2 Thessalonians 2:1-12

Paul's letter highlights the second coming of the Lord is a future event, for some people in his day were falsely claiming Jesus had already returned. Paul indicated the major signs preceding Jesus' return were as follows: One, many Christians in the church would reject Christ. Two, Satan will sit in Solomon's Temple in Jerusalem and declare himself to be God. (Jesus also had said this would occur (Mt 24). It should be noted that in order for Satan to sit in Solomon's Temple in Jerusalem the temple will have to be rebuilt, since it doesn't exist today. The construction of this building in Israel is a major sign to watch for on the nightly news!) Three, there will be a great delusion deceiving many from believing the truth of God.

The book of *Daniel* educated the early church and us today that when the anti-christ (Satan) rises to power he will bring so called "peace" to a very troubled world. The "peace" will last for three and a half years and then abruptly, everything will change. Satan will break the peace treaty, demanding everyone to worship Him. This period on the earth will experience pain and anguish unlike any time period in history, which is described in the book of *Revelation*. The disastrous 10 plagues of Egypt will seem insignificantly small in comparison. Today, the church has a variety of opinions about the end times. Some people consider the subject important and others do not. There are theological positions leading groups to take the positions they have, but since Jesus put much emphasis on this subject in the Scriptures, I believe the end times should be taught with regularity!

The church has yet to experience the end time period the Scriptures foretell. *The Gospel Octagon* holds the position the end is very, very near and Jesus' return will occur in this century, but only time will tell to see if my opinion on this subject is true. Until then, the church should be wisely heeding Jesus' words and watching for the signs of His swift return!

> *But of that day and that hour knoweth no man, no, not the angels which are in heaven, neither the Son, but the Father. Take ye heed, watch and pray: for ye know not when the time is. For the Son of Man is as a man taking a far journey, who left his house, and gave authority to his servants, and to every man his work, and commanded the porter to watch. Watch ye therefore: for ye know not when the master of the house cometh, at even, or at midnight, or at the cockcrowing, or in the morning: Lest coming suddenly he find you sleeping. And what I say unto you I say unto all, Watch.*
>
> *Mark 13:32-37*

Jesus couldn't have been clearer regarding His 2nd coming; He did not reveal the day or the hour, but we are to watch for the signs. When we see them we will know He is near! How can you watch for signs the Scriptures warn about if you don't know them? Having knowledge about the end times is extremely important. *Jesus is returning again soon* and those diligently watching will be joyfully prepared when He does reappear into the world He created!

Chapter Six

JESUS' 2ND COMING

"I saw in the night visions, and, behold, one like the Son of man came with the clouds of heaven, and came to the Ancient of days, and they brought him near before him. And there was given him dominion, and glory, and a kingdom, that all people, nations, and languages, should serve him: his dominion is an everlasting dominion, which shall not pass away, and his kingdom that which shall not be destroyed."

Daniel 7:13-14

The Story Line

Jesus' 2nd coming is the *second* climax of God's storyline! During Jesus' earthly ministry (the first climax) He explained how He would return during the end times to judge the wicked and rescue the righteous (2 Th 1:7-10). In our world the church is eagerly watching and waiting for Jesus' 2nd coming to occur. The story line continues unfolding in our present day, but God has divine wisdom, and knew the end of this story before He ever spoke creation into existence on day one.

Prophecy

During His earthly ministry, Jesus prophesied about His triumphant return to the earth. He pledged after the tribulation comes upon the whole earth, He would again physically step onto the scene, revealing Himself as the King of all kings! The first time Jesus entered the world, He did so in a miraculous way as a babe through a virgin woman. The second time He enters, He will miraculously ride a white horse in the clouds of heaven! Jesus foretold this event when He said,

> *...they [the world] shall see the Son of man coming in the clouds of heaven with power and great glory. And he shall send his angels with a great sound of a trumpet, and they shall gather together his elect from the four winds, from one end of heaven to the other.*

> *Matthew 24:30-31*

When Jesus spoke about His 2nd coming He compared it to the days of Noah saying,

> *For as in the days that were before the flood they were eating and drinking, marrying and giving in marriage, until the day that Noe [Noah] entered into the ark, And knew not until the flood came, and took them all away; so shall also the coming of the Son of man be.*

> *Matthew 24:38-39*

In this passage Jesus explained that just as most people did not believe the flood was coming in Noah's day, so also most will not believe He is returning in the clouds of heaven. Peter also warned about the unbelief of this climatic event when he wrote, *"...there shall come in the last days scoffers, walking after their own lusts, And saying, Where is the promise of his coming? for since the fathers fell asleep, all things continue as they were from the beginning of the creation" (2 Pt 3:3-4).* Unlike the masses who doubt God's Word today, Peter was faithful, like Noah, in warning about God's judgement. Paul was also faithful in reminding his apprentice, Timothy, about Jesus' 2nd coming, to whom he penned the following words:

> *For the grace of God that bringeth salvation hath appeared to all men, Teaching us that, denying ungodliness and worldly lusts, we should live soberly, righteously, and godly, in this present world; Looking for that blessed hope, and the glorious appearing of the great God and our Saviour Jesus Christ; Who gave himself for us, that he might redeem us from all iniquity, and purify unto himself a peculiar people, zealous of good works. These things speak, and exhort, and rebuke with all authority. Let no man despise thee.*

Timothy 2:12-15

Paul's letter reminded Timothy Jesus was returning soon. He encouraged him to think about our Savior's return, for His appearing would remove all pain and suffering from His beloved, faithful children. As well, the author of the book of *Hebrews* encouraged his readers Christ would return soon for those faithful to Him (Hb 9:28). The disciples were excited about Jesus' return because they knew when He appears in the clouds, those faithful to Him would *"receive a crown of glory that fadeth not away" (1 Pt 5:4).*

Throughout history the church has rejoiced at the thought of Jesus' return! This glorious event truly is the hope of every born-again believer in Christ, for this world is not our home. When Jesus comes back to the earth He is going to crush His enemies, but most importantly, He is going to rescue His children from this fallen world!

Jesus Rescues His Children

At the time of the end, Jesus is going to rescue His children from the terrible plagues coming upon the whole earth. This rescue mission is a separate event from Jesus 2nd Coming, but is often tied together with it because both events occur in close proximity to one another. Jesus unveiled to Paul and John how this glorious deliverance would come about. In a letter to the church of Thessalonica, Paul encouraged the believers writing,

> *For this we say unto you by the word of the Lord, that we*
> *which are alive and remain unto the coming of the Lord*
> *shall not prevent them which are asleep. For the Lord*
> *himself shall descend from heaven with a shout, with the*
> *voice of the archangel, and with the trump of God: and*
> *the dead in Christ shall rise first: Then we which are*
> *alive and remain shall be caught up together with them*
> *in the clouds, to meet the Lord in the air: and so shall we*
> *ever be with the Lord.*

1 Thessalonians 4:15-17

Paul's words to the church brought to light the reality that one day the church, at the time of the end, will be caught up in the air by the command of the Lord to enter into His beautiful, grace-filled presence. The words "caught up" come from the original Greek word *harpazo,* meaning to seize or snatch away.[79] When the Bible was translated from Greek to Latin in the early fifth century A.D. the word *rapio* was used, which is why people today speak of this marvelous event using the English word *rapture.*[80] John too recorded this hopeful day in greater detail by recording Jesus' words,

> *And I looked, and behold a white cloud, and upon the*
> *cloud one sat like unto the Son of man, having on his*
> *head a golden crown, and in his hand a sharp sickle. And*
> *another angel came out of the temple, crying with a loud*
> *voice to him that sat on the cloud, Thrust in thy sickle,*
> *and reap: for the time is come for thee to reap; for the*
> *harvest of the earth is ripe. And he that sat on the cloud*
> *thrust in his sickle on the earth; and the earth was*
> *reaped.*

Revelation 14:13-16

In this passage Jesus is referencing the event of the rapture He had previously revealed to Paul. In *Revelation* 15 Jesus uncovers to John the beautiful song sung by those Jesus has rescued and *caught up* unto Himself. The lyrics to this song of heartfelt praise goes,

> *...Great and marvellous are thy works, Lord God Almighty; just and true are thy ways, thou King of saints. Who shall not fear thee, O Lord, and glorify thy name? for thou only art holy: for all nations shall come and worship before thee; for thy judgments are made manifest.*

Revelation 15:3-4

God's children will be overwhelmed with grateful joy, being rescued from the wicked ways of the earth, and being ushered into the splendor-filled majesty of God's Kingdom. This is why the redeemed are found singing this new song full of rejoicing for the wonderful salvation their Lord has granted.

Jesus Crushes His Enemies

On the victorious day of the Lord's triumphant return, the majority of the world will be infected with a deep and festering hatred for everything about Him and for all who follow after Him. But this comes as no surprise to the King of kings. His patience, mercy, and justice are perfect and enduring, but the time for punishment is now at hand. This time Jesus will return to the earth mounted on a white horse in the clouds, ready to *"make war"* against His enemies (Rv 19:11). John beheld Jesus in this revelation and describes Him as looking quite different than when He'd made His first entrance into the world as a babe. John said, The Lord's *"...eyes were as a flame of fire, and on his head were many crowns; and he had a name written, that no man knew, but he himself. And he was clothed with a vesture dipped in blood: and his name is called The Word of God" (Rv 19:12-13).* Jesus is not alone, for *"...the armies which were in heaven followed him upon white horses" (Rv 19:14).* This multitude, however, doesn't wield swords, for their King fights for them! He will cut down His enemies with a sword which will come out of His mouth. The prophet Isaiah and the apostle John both have described and compared this war of destruction during Jesus' 2nd coming as "treading the winepress" (Is 63:3; Rv 19:15). In ancient times, people would tread upon grapes in a winepress, crushing the fruit and spilling its juice so it could be made into wine. When Isaiah and John prophesied Jesus would tread the winepress, they were describing how Jesus would crush the wicked, spilling their life's blood, just like grapes are crushed when one treads upon them in a winepress. John's prophecy dates back to about 90 A.D.[81] Isaiah originally penned his prophecy about 700 years before Jesus was born.[82] Isaiah wrote the following on this subject:

> *Who is this that cometh from Edom, with dyed garments from Bozrah? this that is glorious in his apparel, travelling in the greatness of his strength? I that speak in righteousness, mighty to save. Wherefore art thou red in thine apparel, and thy garments like him that treadeth in the winefat? I have trodden the winepress alone; and of the people there was none with me: for I will tread them in mine anger, and trample them in my fury; and their blood shall be sprinkled upon my garments, and I will stain all my raiment. For the day of vengeance is in mine heart, and the year of my redeemed is come. And I looked, and there was none to help; and I wondered that there was none to uphold: therefore mine own arm brought salvation unto me; and my fury, it upheld me. And I will tread down the people in mine anger, and make them drunk in my fury, and I will bring down their strength to the earth.*
>
> *Isaiah 63:1-6*

As Isaiah witnessed this vision, he became confused, so he inquired of God why His garments were stained red. God answered, telling Isaiah His garments were stained red with the blood of His enemies whom He had crushed.

One day soon God is going to fulfill these prophetic words just as He fulfilled the prophetic words about Himself during His 1st coming to the earth. The wicked did not believe His Words when He spoke with them face to face, nor did they believe Him after He miraculously arose from the dead! Likewise, they will again reject Him and His ways when He descends from the clouds of heaven ready to make all things new (Lk 16:27-31).

Following John's vision about the end time battle, he gives further details about the scene of this hope-filled day of Jesus' 2nd coming when he wrote,

> *And I saw an angel standing in the sun; and he cried with a loud voice, saying to all the fowls that fly in the midst of heaven, Come and gather yourselves together unto the supper of the great God; That ye may eat the flesh of kings, and the flesh of captains, and the flesh of mighty men, and the flesh of horses, and of them that sit on them, and the flesh of all men, both free and bond, both small and great. And I saw the beast, and the kings of the earth, and their armies, gathered together to make war against him that sat on the horse, and against his army. And the beast was taken, and with him the false prophet that wrought miracles before him, with which he deceived them that had received the mark of the beast, and them that worshipped his image. These both were cast alive into a lake of fire burning with brimstone. And the remnant were slain with the sword of him that sat upon the horse, which sword proceeded out of his mouth: and all the fowls were filled with their flesh.*

> *Revelation 19:15-21*

God painted for John a graphic picture of the slaughtering of His enemies. The Lord is going to use the birds to clean the earth of those slain who had unwillingly refused to turn from their sin and bow to their Creator and Savior. Jesus' *Revelation* about the end times and His 2nd coming is so out-of-this world that many Christians today do not believe what the Scriptures foretell, just as they refuse to believe His account of creation. But those who believe Jesus' *Revelation* will be counted as faithful by The Creator. The day of

His return is approaching quickly! **Have you repented of your sin and put your faith in Jesus Christ? If you were to die tonight, do you have confidence, according to the Gospel, where you will be?** (If you do not have confidence you will be with the Lord when you die, please re-read the Evangelistic Answer on pages 4-6.)

Often when God spoke to His prophets about distant future events He didn't reveal the whole story but only a piece, yet, once the 66 books of the Bible were compiled, any studious student has had the ability to seamlessly sew the patches together to form God's glorious storyline, as we hope *The Gospel Octagon* is helping you to do!

God is coming soon to crush His enemies, those rejecting Him as Creator, Savior, Lord, and King. The kings of the earth will gather together to fight Him and Jesus' garments will be stained red with blood from their defeat. The birds throughout the earth will fill the skies converging on the battle scene where the wicked are trodden. Once this battle commences, Jesus will transition the earth for the next major stage of His plot, The Millennial Kingdom!

Chapter Seven

MILLENNIAL KINGDOM

*"Blessed and holy is he that hath part in the first resur-
rection: on such the second death hath no power, but
they shall be priests of God and of Christ, and shall reign
with him a thousand years."*

Revelation 20:6

The Story Line

After crushing His enemies, God will lock Satan up in chains amidst
burning flames. Jesus will then establish Himself as King on the
earth for 1,000 years. This Millennial Kingdom is a mysterious part
of God's script that is quite fascinating! We don't have a full picture
of this time period, but we can glean some very exciting aspects of
what life will be like during this part of God's divine storyline!

One Thousand Years

When God had created Adam and Eve on the sixth day, before sin entered the world, He would walk with them in the midst of the Garden of Eden. There was no pain, suffering, hurt, or heartache. Truth and Peace ruled the land. God was King; The One Adam and Eve looked to for all their needs. Prior to their rebellion, mankind possessed a beautiful, face-to-face relationship with his Maker, unlike our modern world. Just like in the beginning, the Millennial Kingdom will resemble the Garden of Eden, yet it will be distinctly different. It will be similar in that God will reign on earth as King. Peace will fill the streets. People will learn from Jesus, the Master Teacher. People will work hard and their efforts will prosper. Furthermore, people will have a choice to follow Jesus or reject His commandments. This time period will be different from the Garden of Eden in that people will eventually die. Also, there will be a mixture of the heavenly (God and His resurrected saints) on earth along with people still living in their regular earthly bodies. This future time period is not heaven, for the Millennial Kingdom will only last for 1,000 years. Let us look at some of the major Scriptures about this fascinating part of God's story! John recorded his vision about this kingdom, writing,

> *And I saw an angel come down from heaven, having the key of the bottomless pit and a great chain in his hand. And he laid hold on the dragon, that old serpent, which is the Devil, and Satan, and bound him a thousand years, And cast him into the bottomless pit, and shut him up, and set a seal upon him, that he should deceive the nations no more, till the thousand years should be fulfilled: and after that he must be loosed a little season. And I saw thrones, and they sat upon them, and judgment was given unto them: and I saw the souls of them that were beheaded for the witness of Jesus, and for the word of God, and which had not worshipped the beast, neither his image, neither had received his mark upon their foreheads, or in their hands; and they lived and reigned with Christ a thousand years. But the rest of the dead lived not again until the thousand years were*

finished. This is the first resurrection. Blessed and holy is he that hath part in the first resurrection: on such the second death hath no power, but they shall be priests of God and of Christ, and shall reign with him a thousand years.

Revelation 20:1-10

This revelation about the Millennial Kingdom is very insightful! First, God discloses that Satan will be cast into hell for its duration, but will then be released at the end of the Millennial Kingdom (we will come back to this at the end of the chapter). Second, we learn the whole earth will be ruled by Jesus and those who were faithful to Him till death during the end times. Third, we learn that everyone else who died will not come to life until after the 1,000 years.

Fourth, we learn God has a purpose for His faithful disciples: They will have leadership roles during this kingdom as priests! But who will they lead? Well, let us look at *Isaiah* 65 to help answer this question.

And I will rejoice in Jerusalem, and joy in my people: and the voice of weeping shall be no more heard in her, nor the voice of crying. There shall be no more thence an infant of days, nor an old man that hath not filled his days: for the child shall die an hundred years old; but the sinner being an hundred years old shall be accursed. And they shall build houses, and inhabit them; and they shall plant vineyards, and eat the fruit of them. They shall not build, and another inhabit; they shall not plant, and another eat: for as the days of a tree are the days of my people, and mine elect shall long enjoy the work of their hands. They shall not labour in vain, nor bring forth for trouble; for they are the seed of the blessed of the Lord, and their offspring with them. And it shall come to pass, that before they call, I will answer; and while they are yet speaking, I will hear. The wolf and the lamb shall feed together, and the lion shall eat straw like the bullock: and dust shall be the serpent's meat. They shall not hurt nor destroy in all my holy mountain, saith the Lord.

Isaiah 65:19-25

In this passage Isaiah reveals more exciting details about God's glorious story! Let's take them one by one. First, Isaiah partially answers our question, Who will Jesus and His priests lead? From Isaiah's prophecy we learn there will be people living along with Jesus and His resurrected saints during this time period, because it says people will die. The Bible is clear people can only die once, so from this we know these are normal people, like you and I, living in a special time (Hb 9:27). These are the people Jesus and His priests will lead! Second, we learn that Isaiah's prophecy can only be about the Millennial Kingdom, because he points out a day is coming when people would live extremely long life spans, like they had for the first 1,000 years of creation. Having insight into God's story line, we can deduce that the only part of God's story Isaiah could be writing about is the Millennial Kingdom, for after the first 1,000 years of earth's history, life-spans dramatically decreased, and in the Eternal Kingdom (heaven) there is no death (1 Tm 1:16). Third, in the Millennial Kingdom people will still have a choice to obey God or sin against Him. God didn't create robots in the Garden of Eden, nor will He in the Millennial Kingdom. People have a free will to reject God's leadership in their lives or worship Him as Savior and King. Fourth, everyone will build their own homes and gardens, not having others do it for them. During this time, people will reap from their efforts the work they put into it. Fifth, people will repopulate the earth. Sixth, God will be on the earth eager to help those who desire Him in their lives. Seventh, animals will live in peace with one another; there will be no more carnivores. Eighth, animals and man will live at peace with each other too! All eight pieces of information from Isaiah's prophecy are beneficial in providing further insight into our exciting future!

To me, the most thrilling reality about the Millennial Kingdom is people will live under the rule of Jesus and His priests, the resurrected Christians. Wow! Okay, so let's put these pieces to-

gether. During this future period of time, God and His faithful followers (those who have heavenly bodies at that time) will rule over
the people who are still fully human! This is incredible! Why does
the church not talk more about this fantastic time period!? Now that
we have learned more about the Millennial Kingdom, one big question remains: Who *exactly* will these people be that Jesus and His
priests will lead during this peculiar part of God's story?

The Gospel Octagon believes there are two possibilities of
who these people will be. Here is each answer briefly described in
the order which seems most likely to occur.

1. The "people" are those who come to believe in Jesus Christ after
   the rapture and they remain alive to witness His 2nd coming.
   They may finally be converted, or they may hear the Gospel being
   preached by the heavenly angel or possibly the 144,000 faithful
   Israelite believers (Rv 7:1-8; 14:1-7).

2. The "people" are the 144,000 Israelite believers Jesus will protect
   during the end times tribulation. He may keep them alive to repopulate the earth during the Millennial Kingdom (Ex 19:3-6, Is
   43:21, Rv 7:1-8; 14:1-5).

The next question one may ask is, What is God's purpose for
writing the Millennial Kingdom into His plot line? This is an excel-
lent question and one that displays God's patient, loving, and merciful character.

Why The Millennial Kingdom?

God's divine story line is full of fresh twists and unexpected
turns as one pages through the Holy Scriptures. The Millennial
Kingdom is no different, for one must wonder, What is God's purpose in this part of His plot? Why does The Lord not move straight
from His 2nd coming to the Eternal Kingdom? Well, God does have
a purpose and we see it partially revealed in John's vision in *Revelation* 20.

*And when the thousand years are expired, Satan shall be
loosed out of his prison, And shall go out to deceive the
nations which are in the four quarters of the earth, Gog,
and Magog, to gather them together to battle: the number of whom is as the sand of the sea. And they went up
on the breadth of the earth, and compassed the camp of
the saints about, and the beloved city: and fire came
down from God out of heaven, and devoured them. And
the devil that deceived them was cast into the lake of fire
and brimstone, where the beast and the false prophet are,
and shall be tormented day and night for ever and ever.*

Revelation 20:7-10

At the beginning of the Millennial Kingdom Satan will be thrown
into prison, but at the end of the kingdom He will be released and
again attempt to deceive all living on the earth. At the end of 1,000
years, the world will be like heaven on earth; A dream world to people today. In the Millennial Kingdom there will be a perfect government which is just and fair, a perfect economy which is prosperous,
a perfect education curriculum teaching truth, and most importantly, a perfect King, who is God, that is ruling His Kingdom
through His perfect love. The people living in this world will live
long ages and have numerous children, filling the earth and learning
from Jesus Himself, the Master Teacher. This is the world Satan will
be released into to deceive those who hate God and His Kingdom,
where Truth reigns. Once Satan is released, he will succeed in deceiving many into following him and going to war against God: The
One who has provided, taught, healed, counseled, and loved all His
children. Satan and all who follow his prideful, antichrist spirit will
be destroyed by their Maker Himself. Praise the Lord, God will ter-
minate Satan's reign of terror by *cast[ing] [that deceiver] into the lake
of fire and brimstone, where the beast and the false prophet are, and shall
be tormented day and night for ever and ever."* So, What is God's purpose in this part of His plot?

In our world today, people often ask the question, Why did God put the tree in the Garden of Eden if He knew Adam and Eve were going to eat its fruit? (This question was answered in Chapter Two on page 43.) The answer to this question is similar to understanding God's purpose in the Millennial Kingdom. God is seeking people who will love Him when they have the opportunity to not love Him. For love is not truly love unless a choice is involved to have one thing over another. God knows at the end of the Millennial Kingdom there will be many living in His paradise who will reject Him and His love. At the same time, there will be others who will cling to God because of His love, when they have the opportunity to reject Him. God is love! He is after people who will love Him alone, when there is the option to reject Him. If there was no option to reject God, then everyone He created would not have a choice, thereby making them robots. God's divine story line shows He does not desire robots, rather, He longs for people who genuinely love Him. Even still, some people struggle with understanding how God could send people to hell. The Millennial Kingdom is going to prove once and for all that people are the ones choosing to go to hell. God's door, the door to His Eternal Kingdom, is wide open for all to enter, but many have rejected Him in their lives on the earth and many will reject Him in their lives during the Millennial Kingdom.

Often times, people confuse passages of Scripture about the Millennial Kingdom with the Eternal Kingdom (heaven). Be careful, they are indeed different parts of God's story. Making the distinction is important in order to see God's story from beginning to end. From the time God created the heavens and the earth He gave Satan limited rule over earth, but **Satan's time is coming to an abrupt end in the near future.** Nevertheless, God has one final intention for Satan at the end of the Millennial Kingdom which will glorify God and give people the free will to choose to love Him or reject His love. Once the 1,000 years are over, God is going to cast Satan into the lake of fire forever and ever and ever! The Eternal Kingdom will then fully commence, the one every born-again Christian is longing for!

Chapter Eight

ETERNAL KINGDOM

*"And there shall be no more curse: but the throne of God and of the Lamb
shall be in it; and his servants shall serve him: And they shall see his face;
and his name shall be in their foreheads. And there shall be no night there;
and they need no candle, neither light of the sun; for the Lord God giveth
them light: and they shall reign for ever and ever."*

Revelation 22:3-5

The Story Line

God concludes His divine story line with beginning the Eternal
Kingdom. The Great Author is now putting into motion another divine story which will be unlike the first, for God's Eternal Kingdom
will never end...

Kingdom Of Heaven

The Eternal Kingdom is the hope of every believer who has ever lived, from Adam to the very last person who chooses to put their faith in Jesus Christ. During Jesus' earthly ministry the Bible records numerous parables where Jesus spoke about the Kingdom of Heaven. He focused many of these parables on those who would and would not enter His heavenly home. After His resurrection, while Jesus was in His Kingdom, He revealed to John significant details concerning our future home. The last two chapters of *Revelation*, the final book of God's story, record John's awe-inspiring vision, specifically, about our eternal residence.

John's vision about our heavenly home begins by describing the future of planet earth. He wrote, *"I saw a new heaven and a new earth: for the first heaven and the first earth were passed away; and there was no more sea" (Rv 21:1).* The earth we currently live on will be in existence all the way through the Millennial Kingdom and then will be replaced! God's new earth will not have oceans. It may resemble what earth looked like before the great flood of Noah's day. John went on to write,

> *And I John saw the holy city, new Jerusalem, coming down from God out of heaven, prepared as a bride adorned for her husband. And I heard a great voice out of heaven saying, Behold, the tabernacle of God is with men, and he will dwell with them, and they shall be his people, and God himself shall be with them, and be their God.*

> *Revelation 21:2-3*

The Kingdom of God will have a capital called the New Jerusalem, named after Israel's capital, Jerusalem, which means "the city of God."[83] God will rule His Kingdom from The New Jerusalem forever and ever and ever! John wrote further, detailing the hope of every Christian,

*And God shall wipe away all tears from their eyes; and
there shall be no more death, neither sorrow, nor crying,
neither shall there be any more pain: for the former
things are passed away. And he that sat upon the throne
said, Behold, I make all things new. And he said unto me,
Write: for these words are true and faithful. And he said
unto me, It is done. I am Alpha and Omega, the beginning and the end. I will give unto him that is athirst of
the fountain of the water of life freely. He that over-
cometh shall inherit all things; and I will be his God, and
he shall be my son. But the fearful, and unbelieving, and
the abominable, and murderers, and whoremongers, and
sorcerers, and idolaters, and all liars, shall have their
part in the lake which burneth with fire and brimstone:
which is the second death.*

Revelation 21:4-8

Sin will be no more! Death will be no more! Pain will be no more!
Sorrow will be no more! Even the memory of sin and the effects of it
will be removed completely! All things will be made new by God
Himself! God is the Author of His story. He began it and He is going
to finish it! Everyone desiring to join God in His Kingdom is welcome, for God welcomes all who bow their knee to Him alone. As
well, those who reject God, He will reject.

John's vision continues with an elaborate description of our
heavenly home, The New Jerusalem, that is sensational! This Kingdom city will be dimensionally different from everything we've
known. The Millennial Kingdom brought with it a mixture of the
heavenly and the earthly. The Eternal Kingdom will be completely
heavenly! A world with no sun or moon, for God's glory radiates the
light for the entire city! A world with no temple, for the Lord is the
temple and the One we will eternally worship. A world with no
night! A world, praise the Lord, with no sin! A world where only
God's children, those written in His book of life, will dwell in peace
and safety forever and ever (Rv 21)!

This stunning vision continues as John describes in detail many physical characteristics of The New Jerusalem. We learn the city has a square perimeter with each side being about 1,400 miles in length. That is, 1,960,000 square miles. In comparison, Texas, the largest state in the U.S.A. is 268,820 square miles. The New Jerusalem will be over seven times larger than the state of Texas! As well, the city has dazzling, jasper colored walls measuring the same in height as the perimeter does in length and width. There are two shapes which can be made from the dimensions of this unearthly city: A cube or a pyramid. Both shapes have a square for their base and both have four equal sides. We won't know until we arrive, but the city may be far larger than 1,960,000 square miles, if the height of the walls are included in our calculation. We don't know but maybe, just maybe, the city will not be like our world where we are all on one level. It might very well be multileveled or something unknown to us today. If so, since the city has walls the same height as they are length, if we do the calculation, the volume size of the city will be 2,744,000,000 cubic miles. Wow! Now that is big! In comparison, the earth has only 197,000,000 square miles on it and only 27% or 53,190,000 square miles of land![84] Not only is the size of the city jaw-dropping, but the physical makeup of the city is really something to get excited about! The walls have 12 foundations in which the 12 apostles' names are inscribed, and each foundation is made of a unique, precious stone. Plus, each wall of the city has three gates, each guarded by an angel. Amazingly, the gates are made of a single pearl. The gates will never be shut, but only God's redeemed children will be permitted to enter, those whose names are recorded in God's book, *"the Lamb's book of life" (Rv 21:27)*. Although the Bible doesn't tell us specifically, the gates are probably massive in size, given the great size of the city walls. God's gates will have the inscription of the 12 tribes of Israel, as an eternal memorial to God's people whom He revealed Himself to in a special way amongst all the people of the world. The rest of the city, even the streets, are made with the purest gold, so pure it is as clear as glass.

As each day passes, the reality of stepping through the pearly gates, onto the streets of gold grows nearer and nearer. John goes on in even greater detail writing,

> *And he shewed [showed] me a pure river of water of life, clear as crystal, proceeding out of the throne of God and of the Lamb. In the midst of the street of it, and on either side of the river, was there the tree of life, which bare twelve manner of fruits, and yielded her fruit every month: and the leaves of the tree were for the healing of the nations.*
>
> *Revelation 22:1-2*

In the Eternal Kingdom there will be a single tree bearing 12 *different* kinds of fruit! Can you believe that!? On earth we know one tree bears one fruit for a short season of the year. In God's city, one tree bears 12 different kinds of fruit every single month forever!!! Are you getting excited yet!? Although John's description of God's Kingdom is lengthy, he really only provides a few details which wet the tastebuds of every true believer, encouraging them to diligently watch and wait with great anticipation for their entrance into our Father's home!

Then, the angel began to close the revelation Jesus gave him by saying,

> *And there shall be no more curse: but the throne of God and of the Lamb shall be in it; and his servants shall serve him: And they shall see his face; and his name shall be in their foreheads. And there shall be no night there; and they need no candle, neither light of the sun; for the Lord God giveth them light: and they shall reign for ever and ever.*
>
> *Revelation 22:3-5*

Praise the Lord! The curse of sin will be removed and we can worship God freely in His Kingdom without persecution from without
and within! God will lead His people to know Him and His Word!
The King will teach and there will no longer be any dissension. The
angel finished speaking to John by saying, *"...These sayings are faithful and true: and the Lord God of the holy prophets sent his angel to shew
[show] unto his servants the things which must shortly be done" (Rv 22:6).*
Then the Lord said, *"Behold, I come quickly: blessed is he that keepeth
the sayings of the prophecy of this book" (Rv 22:7).* After John saw and
heard this vision he wrote, *"...I fell down to worship before the feet of
the angel which shewed [showed] me these things" (Rv 22:8).* At that, the
angel gave John a stark warning saying, *"See thou do it not: for I am
thy fellowservant, and of thy brethren the prophets, and of them which keep
the sayings of this book: worship God" (Rv 22:9).* As John's revelation
from the angel came to a close, the Lord himself continued to speak.
The apostle recorded the words of Jesus in the last nine verses of the
Bible, in which Jesus said,

> *I am Alpha and Omega, the beginning and the end, the
> first and the last. Blessed are they that do his command-
> ments, that they may have right to the tree of life, and
> may enter in through the gates into the city. For without
> are dogs, and sorcerers, and whoremongers, and mur-
> derers, and idolaters, and whosoever loveth and maketh
> a lie. I Jesus have sent mine angel to testify unto you
> these things in the churches. I am the root and the off-
> spring of David, and the bright and morning star. And
> the Spirit and the bride say, Come. And let him that
> heareth say, Come. And let him that is athirst come. And
> whosoever will, let him take the water of life freely. For I
> testify unto every man that heareth the words of the
> prophecy of this book, If any man shall add unto these
> things, God shall add unto him the plagues that are writ-
> ten in this book: And if any man shall take away from the
> words of the book of this prophecy, God shall take away
> his part out of the book of life, and out of the holy city,
> and from the things which are written in this book. He
> which testifieth these things saith, Surely I come quickly.*

Amen. Even so, come, Lord Jesus. The grace of our Lord
Jesus Christ be with you all. Amen.

Revelation 22:13-21

God not only began His story, but is going to end His story by beginning another! Throughout the Scriptures The Lord reminds His
people to obey His commandments. Those who are faithful to Jesus
will be ushered into the Kingdom of God, their eternal home.
Whereas, those who reject the truth of God's Word will not enter,
but will be cast into the lake of fire forever. Jesus blessed the church
with His *Revelation* so we would know what to expect during the
end times, have a greater understanding about the Millennial Kingdom, and to encourage our hearts and minds with the reality that
one day soon God's faithful children will inherit His Kingdom that
will never, ever end! The pearly gates of heaven are open to all who
will come, but their is a requirement to enter: One's sins *must* be
washed by the blood of Jesus, the sacrificial Lamb, who died and
rose again on the third day, breaking the curse of sin that leads to
eternal death in exchange for eternal life.

Jesus concluded His *Revelation* saying that those who add
to or take away from any of His Words will be severely judged. The
Bible is the most fascinating story of all time! Each divine detail has
been providentially written by God Himself, the Author of Life! In
His last words to John, Jesus reminded the church He is coming
quickly, so His church should be watching, ready, and waiting for
His soon return.

Once the Eternal Kingdom begins, the end of God's
divine story line will come to an exciting conclusion, with
the most breathtaking story that ever was or ever will be
written! One could not dream up this grand, monumental, stunning story God has written.**This astounding plot causes one to**

ponder what wonders God has prepared for those who love Him in His Eternal Kingdom, the Kingdom of Heaven!

CONCLUSION

God's story has not yet ended, but the Author of Life certainly knows, and has revealed its magnificent finale to the whole world through His Holy Scriptures, the 66 books of the Bible. As I mentioned in the Introduction of this book, **The purpose of *The Gospel Octagon* is to teach an overview of the one story being told in the Bible you and I are still living out.** God's Word is lengthly but we can know and understand the details better when we have a clear picture of His story line from beginning to end.

Sometimes people can get lost in the midst of the BIG story God has written. Did you know even some of Jesus' disciples did not understand God's story, but were *only* focused on what was in front of their eyes? In *Luke* 24 we learn how two of Jesus' disciples got lost within the bigness of God's divine story line. Their small, yet important, interaction with Jesus goes like this:

Two of Jesus' disciples were on a seven mile journey walking from Jerusalem to the village of Emmaus, three days after Jesus' crucifixion. On their journey they conversed about the amazing events surrounding the death of Christ. Unexpectedly, the resurrected Christ approached them, but God closed their eyes from perceiving His identity. As Jesus walked in their company He asked them, *"What manner of communications are these that ye have one to another, as ye walk, and are sad" (Lk 24:17)*? The two disciples explained to Jesus what they were talking about; They were talking about Him! After they finished explaining their conversation, Jesus rebuked them for disbelieving all that the prophets had written about the Messiah. Jesus said, *"...O fools, and slow of heart to believe all that the prophets have spoken: Ought not Christ to have suffered these things, and to enter into his glory" (Lk 24:25-26)*? Jesus was disappointed His disciples hadn't believed the account of the prophets. The next verse records that *"...beginning at Moses and all the prophets, he expounded unto them in **all the scriptures** the things concerning himself" (Lk 24:27)*. Upon reaching their destination they pleaded with Him to stay with them that evening. He obliged and broke bread with them. After Jesus prayed over the meal, God opened the eyes of the two men and they realized it was Jesus sitting with them! At that moment He disappeared! *"And they said one to another, Did not our heart burn within us, while he talked with us by the way, and while he opened to us the scriptures" (Lk 24:32)*? Abruptly after Jesus vanished, these two men trekked the seven mile journey back to Jerusalem in the night hours and found the disciples gathered together. They recounted the astonishing news of how they had walked and learned from the resurrected Christ that afternoon and how He had disappeared before their very eyes! Then suddenly Jesus appeared among them in the locked room as the two men were giving their testimony, terrifying everyone, for they thought He was a ghost! He reassured them He was real by exposing to them the scars of crucifixion on His body and eating a meal with them. Over the meal He reminded them,

> *...These are the words which I spake [spoke] unto you, while I was yet with you, that all things must be fulfilled, which were written in the law of Moses, and in the prophets, and in the psalms, concerning me. Then opened he their understanding, that they might understand the scriptures, And said unto them, Thus it is writ-*

*ten, and thus it behooved Christ to suffer, and to rise
from the dead the third day: And that repentance and
remission of sins should be preached in his name among
all nations, beginning at Jerusalem. And ye are witnesses
of these things.*

Luke 24:44-48

The death of Jesus brought much confusion and disappointment to
His disciples, but Jesus unfolded to them how the books of Moses,
the prophets and *Psalms* had foretold and explained His purpose,
coming, death, and resurrection. After hearing and comprehending
the full picture, the disciples were filled with great joy! They now
clearly understood God's perfect redemption story, and why Jesus
had to die and rise from the grave three days later to break the curse
of sin. Likewise, **when God's disciples today have a clear picture of His divine story line, it excites us to live for God
and share the Gospel with every creature (Mk 16:15)!**

THE NEXT STEP!

I hope *The Gospel Octagon* has helped you learn an overview of the one story God is telling all people! Now that you have a clear understanding of the Scriptures, I encourage you to take your next step in learning more about God's Word, and who you were created to be as a son or daughter of The King! **Your next step is to read the Bible!** You are a part of God's divine story line! Reading the Bible on a regular basis will help you to know more intimately the One who fashioned you.

I hope you have put your faith in Jesus Christ for the forgiveness of your sins which have separated you from Him. (Please re-read The Evangelistic Answer on pages 4-6 to learn how to have your sins forgiven, escape hell and inherit eternal life in heaven.) **God's love is amazing!** He displayed how much He loves you by paying your fine on the cross with His own blood. If you love Him, you will seek to know Him more through His revelation to you in His Holy Word, The Bible!

May our Creator and Savior reveal Himself to you more and more as you seek to know who He is, and who He created you to be in this world and in eternity!

Appendix I

COVENANTS

A covenant is a legally binding contract or agreement. "The Bible is a covenant document."[85] Throughout the Bible there are six clear covenants between God and man.

The Garden of Eden

The first covenant began in the Garden of Eden in *Genesis* 2. The agreement was simple. God created man and woman to enjoy The Lord's creation and there was one binding agreement. *Genesis* 2:16 says,

> *And the Lord God commanded the man, saying, Of every tree of the garden thou mayest freely eat: But of the tree of the knowledge of good and evil, thou shalt not eat of it: for in the day that thou eatest thereof thou shalt surely die.*

The covenant was composed of one command. Live by the covenant and you live. Reject the covenant and you die. We all know what happened there...

Noah

The second covenant God made was with Noah. After God destroyed the earth with a world-wide flood, He made a covenant with Noah and all life on earth. The agreement was that God would never again destroy the world by water. God created the rainbow as a sign in the heavens that would remind all life of God's faithfulness to His covenant (Gn 6:18-21; 9:1-3).

Abraham

The third covenant God made was with Abraham. This agreement had specific personal blessing over Abraham and his descendants. The covenant regarded a new name (Abraham), promise of descendants, and land. The sign of the agreement was that each male associated with Abraham's people had to be circumcised. Circumcision was a sign of obedience that set apart the covenant people of God (Gn 15:1-18; 17:1-14).

Moses

The fourth covenant God made was with Moses and all the Israelites. The agreement was that the Israelites would only follow God alone and no gods made up in the imaginations of men. In the covenant God put forth over 600 laws for His people to follow. The laws included civil, temple, social, and moral commands that were part of this agreement. In summary God said, "Obey me and all will go well for you. Reject me and all will go bad." The people said they would obey (Ex 6:2-8; 19:3-6; 34:27).

David

The fifth covenant God made was with king David, of Israel. This covenant was that the descendants of David would have an everlasting kingdom (2 Sa 7:5-29; Ps 89:3-4).

The Church

The six covenant God made was with the church. This covenant is wholly different than the others. This time, God came into the world He created as a babe. He grew up in the world He created. He taught truth in the world He created. Then He was murdered by the people He created, whom He had made the previous covenants with. Then after three days He rose from the grave, defeating sin and death, and sealing this new covenant with His people, the one's who believed in Him by faith. The covenant was for the forgiveness of sin. Those who humbled themselves by putting their faith in Jesus would have their sins forgiven and would escape God's holy wrath that is coming upon all humanity because of sin. Since their sins would be forgiven, they would inherit eternal life in the Kingdom of God (Hb 8:8-13; 12:24).

Appendix II

THE SABBATH

When God gave the Israelites the 10 Commandments, He included the fourth commandment, which is to observe the Sabbath. The commandment reads,

> *Remember the sabbath day, to keep it holy. Six days shalt thou labour, and do all thy work: But the seventh day is the sabbath of the Lord thy God: in it thou shalt not do any work, thou, nor thy son, nor thy daughter, thy manservant, nor thy maidservant, nor thy cattle, nor thy stranger that is within thy gates: For in six days the Lord made heaven and earth, the sea, and all that in them is, and rested the seventh day: wherefore the Lord blessed the sabbath day, and hallowed it.*

Exodus 20:8-11

The fourth commandment was given to the Israelites for a weekly reminder to rest and focus on God, while remembering all things were created by The Lord in six days.

Today, Christians are not sinning if they do not observe the Sabbath. Observing the weekly Sabbath was a requirement for Jews, but since Jesus created a new covenant for His people to follow, Christians are not required to keep the Sabbath day. Paul wrote about this subject to the church of Colosse when he penned the following words, *"Let no man therefore judge you in meat, or in drink, or in respect of an holyday, or of the new moon, or of the sabbath days" (Co 2:16).* Christians are not required to observe the Sabbath, just as we are not required to follow the Jewish dietary laws (Rm 14:5-6).

With that said, Christians are required to obey the moral commands God gave the Israelites. Christians are not saved by observing the moral commands, we are saved by putting our faith in Jesus Christ (Ep 2:8). When an individual puts their faith in Christ alone for the forgiveness of their sins, Jesus' righteousness becomes the righteousness of each born-again Christian (Jn 3:3; 1 Co 1:30; 2 Co 5:21; Ga 2:16; Ph 3:9). However, if a Christian is truly born-again they will strive with a joyful heart to live righteously, for the Holy Spirit dwelling within each believer will guide them to honor and obey Him (Rm 8:1-4; Ga 2:20; 1 Pt 2:24).

Appendix III

JESUS' GENEALOGY

The Bible records Jesus' prophetic genealogy in both *Matthew* 1:1-17 and *Luke* 3:23-38. These two genealogical records are interesting when looked at side by side. Let us take a closer look at both records.

Matthew's Record

Matthew's record starts with Abraham and goes forward to Jesus. Matthew breaks down the genealogy into three sets of 14 because he highlighted Jesus is a descendant of King David to his Jewish audience (This is the best explanation I've heard). In Hebrew each letter of the alphabet is represented by a number. For example, "David" in Hebrew is *Dvd*. The "d" equals four and the "v" equals six. So, two "d's" plus one "v" equals 14, which is the number of King David's name. So, the reason Matthew broke Jesus' genealogy into three sets of 14 was to shout in written form to his Jewish audience that their Messiah, the one the prophets spoke and wrote about, had come in the life of Jesus Christ. Due to Matthew's intentions, he purposely left some people out of the genealogy to drive his point home.

Luke's Record

Luke's genealogical record starts with Jesus and goes backward all the way to the Garden of Eden when God created Adam. Luke appears to include every person in Jesus lineage.

Both Matthew and Luke follow the same lineage up until King David's sons, then they change! The likely reason for the change is Matthew follows Solomon (Mary's lineage) and Luke follows Nathan (Joseph's lineage).[86] The Bible records the Messiah would come from the lineage of King David and it is powerful to note that both Joseph and Mary were direct descendants of Israel's second king.

GOD'S DIVINE STORYLINE

Creation

God introduces His story by testifying of His Creation account. The introduction of the plot is all about God creating the heaven's, the earth, and all He put on the earth. Undoubtedly, this section of God's story has been hijacked more than any other. The Creation section is the foundation of the rest of this book and it is truly the foundation of the Gospel of Jesus Christ.

Man's Sin

After God introduces His story by testifying of His Creation account, the rising action of the plot follows, including both this chapter and the next about Israel. From here, the plot intensifies. This section focuses on the origin of sin and its escalation throughout God's story.

Israel

Two thousand and forty nine years after the creation of the heavens and the earth, God's man, Abraham, came into the picture. God chose Abraham and His descendants to build a nation, a people, whom He would reveal Himself to, so they would obey Him and inform the world about the truth of God. The Israelite's were unique in all the earth, they were the only nation God formed to reveal Himself to so one day He could make Himself known to every person He created!

Jesus' 1st Coming

In eternity past, God's plan for the climax of His story was to be when He became a human in Jesus Christ. God became a human to redeem people from the curse of sin, and offer them eternal life. When mankind rebelled against God by breaking His law, God in His justice had to be faithful to the eternal laws which are part of His pure, holy kingdom. That meant that after man died physically he would have to be eternally separated from God because God is perfect and can not have fellowship with anyone who is not perfect too. Therefore, God chose to come into the world He created to defeat the curse of sin, so that men could be made right with their Creator, once again!

The Church

After the climax of the death and resurrection of Jesus Christ, God created the church to proclaim His Gospel message of light and truth in a world of darkness and lies. The church began 2,000 years ago on God's story line, but we are still at this part in the plot today. The church includes Jewish and Gentile (non Jewish) believers in Christ. For Jewish believers in God, the church is a continuation of their faith under God's new covenant. For Gentile believers in God, their faith is grafted into the branch of the Israelites, for they are the people whom God created for Himself.

Jesus' 2nd Coming

Jesus' 2nd coming is the *second* climax of God's storyline! During Jesus' earthly ministry (the first climax) He explained how He would return during the end times to judge the wicked and rescue

the righteous (2 Th 1:7-10). In our world the church is eagerly
watching and waiting for Jesus' 2nd coming to occur. The story line
continues unfolding in our present day, but God has divine wisdom,
and knew the end of this story before He ever spoke creation into
existence on day one.

Millennial Kingdom

After crushing His enemies, God will lock Satan up in chains amidst
burning flames. Jesus will then establish Himself as King on the
earth for 1,000 years. This Millennial Kingdom is a mysterious part
of God's script that is quite fascinating! We don't have a full picture
of this time period, but we can glean some very exciting aspects of
what life will be like during this part of God's divine storyline!

Eternal Kingdom

God concludes His divine story line with beginning the Eternal
Kingdom. The Great Author is now putting into motion another divine story which will be unlike the first, for God's Eternal Kingdom
will never end...

BIBLIOGRAPHY

. "Ancient Jewish History: The Two Kingdoms." Retrieved December 26, 2015, from http://www.jewishvirtuallibrary.org/jsource/History/Kingdoms1.html.

. "The Cells in Your Body." Retrieved January 5, 2016, from http://sciencenetlinks.com/student-teacher-sheets/cells-your-body/.

. "Dinosaur." Retrieved January 30, 2016, from https://www.dropbox.com/sh/gj5xbu6v095w519/AAD5aKZuZOZxPloq4IOjdubJa/Charts%2C%20Figures%2C%20Illustrations?dl=0&preview=Dreadnoughtus+Size+%26+Weight+Comparision+(LBS)+JPG.jpg.

(1986). The Incredible Machine. The National Geographic, The National Geographic Society.

(2016). Merriam-Webster. merriam-webster.com.

Bergman, J. (1984). "Mankind-The Pinnacle of God's Creation." Acts & Facts 13(7).

Bert Thompson, P. D. "Biblical Accuracy and Circumcision on the 8th Day." Retrieved December 27, 2015, from http://www.apologeticspress.org/APContent.aspx?category=13&article=1118.

Bing.com. (2015). "Bing Maps." Retrieved December, 4, 2015.

Brown, F., Samuel Rolles Driver, and Charles Augustus Briggs (1977). Enhanced Brown-Driver-Briggs Hebrew and English Lexicon. Logos.

Chad, B. (2003). Holman Illustrated Bible Dictionary. Logos Holman Bible Publishers.

Chad, B. (2003). Holman Illustrated Bible Dictonary, Holman Bible Publishers.

Constable, D. T. L. (2015 Edition). "Notes on Genesis." Retrieved July 2015, 2015.

Ewing, R. (2014). "Drexel Team Unveils Dreadnoughtus: A Gigantic, Exceptionally Complete Sauropod Dinosaur." 2016, from http://drexel.edu/now/archive/2014/September/Dreadnoughtus-Dinosaur/.

Genesis, A. I. "Adam + Eve = All Skin Tones?" Retrieved May, 12, 2015, from https://answersingenesis.org/racism/adam-eve-all-skin-tones/.

Gilbert, G. D. (2010). What is the Gospel? Wheaton, Illnois, Crossway.

Gitt, D. W. (1989). "Information: The Third Fundamental Quantity." Siemens Review 56(6).

Ham, K. (2012). The Lie: Evolution/Millions of Years. Green Forest, AR, New Leaf Publishing Group, Inc.

Henry M. Morris, P. D. (1973). "Evolution, Creation, and the Public Schools." Acts & Facts 2(1).

Henry M. Morris, P. D. (1991). "Adam to the Animals." Acts & Facts 20(2).

Hovind, E. (2014). "Scientists Discover Behemoth."

Howell, E. (2104). "How Many Galaxies Are There?", from http://www.space.com/25303-how-many-galaxies-are-in-the-universe.ht ml.

III, H. M. (2008). Exploring the Evidence for Creation. Eugene, Oregon, Harvest House.

James J.S. Johnson, J. D., Th.D. (2015). "Sound Science About Dinosaurs." Acts & Facts 44(1).

James, S. (1997). Dictionary of Biblical Languages with Semantic Domains: Greek (New Testament). Logos Research Sysytems, Inc.

Jason Lisle, P. D. (2013). "The Solar System: Earth and Moon." Acts & Facts 42(10).

Jeffery P. Tomkins, P. D. (2015). "Three-Dimensional DNA Code Defies Evolution." Retrieved January 5, 2016, from http://www.icr.org/article/8691/282/.

Jerry Bergman, P. D. (2015). "Creation Converstion: From Atheist to Creationist." Acts & Facts 44(2).

John D. Morris, P. D. (2005). "Dinosaur Soft Parts." Acts & Facts 34: 6.

Kaufmann Kohler, J. L. M. (2016). "JewishEncyclopedia.com." Retrieved January 4, 2016, from http://jewishencyclopedia.com/articles/12012-pentecost.

Loveett, K. H. a. T. (2007). "Was There Really a Noah's Ark & Flood?" Retrieved January 30, 2016, from https://answersingenesis.org/the-flood/global/was-there-really-a-noahs-a rk-flood/.

Lovett, T. (2007). Thinking Outside the Box. Answers Magazine. answersingenesis.org, answersingenesis.

Manser, M. H. (2009). Dictionary of Bible Themes: The Accessible and Comprehensive Tool for Topical Studies. London.

method, s. (2014). Collins English Dictionary. Dictionary.com, HarperCollins

Morris, D. H. M. (2006). "The New Defender's Study Bible." Retrieved July 3, 2015, from http://www.icr.org/bible/Exodus/12/37.

Morris, D. H. M. (2006). "The New Defender's Study Bible Notes." from http://www.icr.org/index.php?module=home&action=submitsearch&f_su bmit=Search&f_context_any=any&section=bible&f_search_type=bible&f _keyword_any=Genesis+32:28.

Morris, D. H. M. (2006). "New Defender's Study Bible Notes." Retrieved July 2, 2015, from http://www.icr.org/bible/Gen/22/1.

Morris, H. M. (1982). "Bible-Believing Scientists of the Past." Acts & Facts 11(1).

Morris, J. W. a. H. (1961). The Genesis Flood. Phillipsburg, New Jersey, Presbyterian and Reformed

Norman L. Geisler, P. B. (2001). Unshakable Foundations. Minneapolis, Minnesota, Bethany House Publisher.

Powell, M. A. (2011). The HarperCollins Bible Dictionary (Revised and Updated). New York, HarperCollins.

Purdom, D. G. (2010). "One Race." Retrieved May, 13, 2015, from https://answersingenesis.org/racism/one-race/.

Richards, L., & Richards, L. O. (1987). The teacher's commentary. Includes index. Wheaton, Ill, Victor Books.

Sailhamer, J. H. (1982). The Expositor's Bible Commentary.

Sharp, T. (2012). "How Big is Earth?" Retrieved December 26, 2015, from http://www.space.com/17638-how-big-is-earth.html.

Sharp, T. (2012). "How Big is the Sun?/Size of the Sun." from http://www.space.com/17001-how-big-is-the-sun-size-of-the-sun.html.

Sherwin, F. (2013). Guide To Animals. Dallas, TX, The Institute of Creation Research.

Slick, M. (2015). "Covenant." Retrieved August 8, 2015, from https://carm.org/christianity/christian-doctrine/covenant.

Smith, C. (2014) "Dinosaur Soft Tissue." Creation Magazine.

Snelling, D. A. A. (2007). High & Dry Sea Creatures. Answers Magazine. answersingenesis.org, answersingenesis.

Tan-Gatue, P. (2015). The Lexham Bible Dictionary. J. D. Barry, Lexham Press.

Thomas, R. L. (1998). New American Standard Hebrew-Aramaic and Greeek dictionaries.

Walter A., E., and Barry J. Beitzel. (1988). Baker enclyclopedia of the Bible, Baker
Book House Company.

Walter A., E., and Barry J. Beitzel. (1988). Baker Encyclopedia of the Bible.

White, M. (2006). "Billions of People in Thousands of Years?" Answers Magizine.

Williams, M. (2014). "10 Facts About The Milky Way." from
http://www.universetoday.com/22285/facts-about-the-milky-way/.

Woetzel, D. "Ancient Dinosaur Depictions." Retrieved January 30, 2016, from
http://www.genesispark.com/exhibits/evidence/historical/ancient/dinosa
ur/.

Woetzel, D. "Cain And Abel." Retrieved August 5, 2015, from
http://www.icr.org/article/18058.

Woetzel, D. "Soft Tissue in Dinosaur Bones." Retrieved January 30, 2016, from
http://www.genesispark.com/exhibits/evidence/paleontological/old-bone
/soft-tissue-in-dinosaur-bones/.

Wood, D. R. W., and I. Howard Marshall (1996). The New Bible Dictionary, Third
Edition. Logos Edition.

Woodmorappe, J. (2013). "How Could Noah Fit the Animlas on the Ark and Care for
Them?" Retrieved July 2, 2015, from
https://answersingenesis.org/noahs-ark/how-could-noah-fit-the-animals-
on-the-ark-and-care-for-them/.

Yeoman, B. (2006). "Schweitzer's Dangerous Discovery." Discover: Science For The
Curious (April).

END NOTES

[1] Gilbert, G. D. (2010). What is the Gospel? Wheaton, Illnois, Crossway.

[2] James, S. (1997). Dictionary of Biblical Languages with Semantic Domains: Greek (New Testament). Logos Research Sysytems, Inc.

[3] Walter A., E., and Barry J. Beitzel. (1988). Baker Encyclopedia of the Bible.

[4] Constable, D. T. L. (2015 Edition). "Notes on Genesis." Retrieved July 2015, 2015.

[5] Sailhamer, J. H. (1982). The Expositor's Bible Commentary.

[6] Ham, K. (2012). The Lie: Evolution/Millions of Years. Green Forest, AR, New Leaf Publishing Group, Inc.

[7] Norman L. Geisler, P. B. (2001). Unshakable Foundations. Minneapolis, Minnesota, Bethany House Publisher.

[8] Henry M. Morris, P. D. (1973). "Evolution, Creation, and the Public Schools." Acts & Facts 2(1).

[9] method, s. (2014). Collins English Dictionary. Dictionary.com, HarperCollins

[10] Morris, H. M. (1982). "Bible-Believing Scientists of the Past." Acts & Facts 11(1).

[11] Ibid.

[12] Ibid.

[13] Ibid.

[14] Ibid.

[15] Ham, K. (2012). The Lie: Evolution/Millions of Years. Green Forest, AR, New Leaf Publishing Group, Inc.

[16] (2016). Merriam-Webster. merriam-webster.com.

[17] James J.S. Johnson, J. D., Th.D. (2015). "Sound Science About Dinosaurs." <u>Acts &</u> <u>Facts</u> **44**(1).

[18] Thomas, R. L. (1998). <u>New American Standard Hebrew-Aramaic and Greeek dictionaries.</u>

[19] Hovind, E. (2014). "Scientists Discover Behemoth."

[20] . "Dinosaur."   Retrieved January 30, 2016, from https://www.dropbox.com/sh/gj5xbu6vo95w519/AAD5aKZuZOZxPloq4IOjdubJa/C harts%2C%20Figures%2C%20Illustrations?dl=0&preview=Dreadnoughtus+Size+%2 6+Weight+Comparision+(LBS)+JPG.jpg.

[21] Ewing, R. (2014). "Drexel Team Unveils Dreadnoughtus: A Gigantic, Exceptionally Complete Sauropod Dinosaur." 2016, from http://drexel.edu/now/archive/2014/September/Dreadnoughtus-Dinosaur/.

[22] Sherwin, F. (2013). <u>Guide To Animals</u>. Dallas, TX, The Institute of Creation Research.

[23] Woetzel, D. "Ancient Dinosaur Depictions."   Retrieved January 30, 2016, from http://www.genesispark.com/exhibits/evidence/historical/ancient/dinosaur/.

[24] Ibid.

[25] Ibid.

[26] Yeoman, B. (2006). "Schweitzer's Dangerous Discovery." <u>Discover: Science For The Curious</u> (April).

[27] Smith, C. (2014) "Dinosaur Soft Tissue." <u>Creation Magazine</u>.

[28] John D. Morris, P. D. (2005). "Dinosaur Soft Parts." <u>Acts & Facts</u> **34**: 6.

[29] Woetzel, D. "Soft Tissue in Dinosaur Bones."   Retrieved January 30, 2016, from http://www.genesispark.com/exhibits/evidence/paleontological/old-bone/soft-tissu e-in-dinosaur-bones/.

[30] Howell, E. (2104). "How Many Galaxies Are There?", from http://www.space.com/25303-how-many-galaxies-are-in-the-universe.html.

[31] Williams, M. (2014). "10 Facts About The Milky Way." from http://www.universetoday.com/22285/facts-about-the-milky-way/.

[32] Sharp, T. (2012). "How Big is the Sun?/Size of the Sun." from http://www.space.com/17001-how-big-is-the-sun-size-of-the-sun.html.

[33] Jason Lisle, P. D. (2013). "The Solar System: Earth and Moon." <u>Acts & Facts</u> **42**(10).

[34] Bergman, J. (1984). "Mankind-The Pinnacle of God's Creation." Ibid. **13**(7).

[35] Jerry Bergman, P. D. (2015). "Creation Converstion: From Atheist to Creationist." Ibid. **44**(2).

[36] Bergman, J. (1984). "Mankind-The Pinnacle of God's Creation." Ibid. **13**(7).

[37] Gitt, D. W. (1989). "Information: The Third Fundamental Quantity." Siemens Review **56**(6).

[38] Bergman, J. (1984). "Mankind-The Pinnacle of God's Creation." Acts & Facts **13**(7).

[39] Gitt, D. W. (1989). "Information: The Third Fundamental Quantity." Siemens Review **56**(6).

[40] (1986). The Incredible Machine. The National Geographic, The National Geographic Society.

[41] . "The Cells in Your Body." Retrieved January 5, 2016, from http://sciencenetlinks.com/student-teacher-sheets/cells-your-body/.

[42] Jeffery P. Tomkins, P. D. (2015). "Three-Dimensional DNA Code Defies Evolution." Retrieved January 5, 2016, from http://www.icr.org/article/8691/282/.

[43] (1986). The Incredible Machine. The National Geographic, The National Geographic Society.

[44] Ibid.

[45] Woetzel, D. "Cain And Abel." Retrieved August 5, 2015, from http://www.icr.org/article/18058.

[46] Ibid.

[47] White, M. (2006). "Billions of People in Thousands of Years?" Answers Magizine.

[48] Morris, J. W. a. H. (1961). The Genesis Flood. Phillipsburg, New Jersey, Presbyterian and Reformed

[49] Lovett, T. (2007). Thinking Outside the Box. Answers Magazine. answersingenesis.org, answersingenesis.

[50] Henry M. Morris, P. D. (1991). "Adam to the Animals." Acts & Facts **20**(2).

[51] Walter A., E., and Barry J. Beitzel. (1988). Baker enclyclopedia of the Bible, Baker Book House Company.

[52] Woodmorappe, J. (2013). "How Could Noah Fit the Animlas on the Ark and Care for Them?" Retrieved July 2, 2015, from https://answersingenesis.org/noahs-ark/how-could-noah-fit-the-animals-on-the-ark-and-care-for-them/.

[53] Ibid.

[54] Loveett, K. H. a. T. (2007). "Was There Really a Noah's Ark & Flood?" Retrieved January 30, 2016, from https://answersingenesis.org/the-flood/global/was-there-really-a-noahs-ark-flood/.

55 Snelling, D. A. A. (2007). High & Dry Sea Creatures. Answers Magazine. answersingenesis.org, answersingenesis.

56 Genesis, A. I. "Adam + Eve = All Skin Tones?" Retrieved May, 12, 2015, from https://answersingenesis.org/racism/adam-eve-all-skin-tones/.

57 Ibid.

58 Purdom, D. G. (2010). "One Race." Retrieved May, 13, 2015, from https://answersingenesis.org/racism/one-race/.

59 Morris, D. H. M. (2006). "New Defender's Study Bible Notes." Retrieved July 2, 2015, from http://www.icr.org/bible/Gen/22/1.

60 Brown, F., Samuel Rolles Driver, and Charles Augustus Briggs (1977). Enhanced Brown-Driver-Briggs Hebrew and English Lexicon. Logos.

61 Manser, M. H. (2009). Dictionary of Bible Themes: The Accessible and Comprehensive Tool for Topical Studies. London.

62 Walter A., E., and Barry J. Beitzel. (1988). Baker Encyclopedia of the Bible.

63 Morris, D. H. M. (2006). "The New Defender's Study Bible Notes." from http://www.icr.org/index.php?module=home&action=submitsearch&f_submit=Search&f_context_any=any&section=bible&f_search_type=bible&f_keyword_any=Genesis+32:28.

64 Morris, D. H. M. (2006). "The New Defender's Study Bible." Retrieved July 3, 2015, from http://www.icr.org/bible/Exodus/12/37.

65 Brown, F., Samuel Rolles Driver, and Charles Augustus Briggs (1977). Enhanced Brown-Driver-Briggs Hebrew and English Lexicon. Logos.

66 Chad, B. (2003). Holman Illustrated Bible Dictionary. Logos Holman Bible Publishers.

67 Wood, D. R. W., and I. Howard Marshall (1996). The New Bible Dictionary, Third Edition. Logos Edition.

68 . "Ancient Jewish History: The Two Kingdoms." Retrieved December 26, 2015, from http://www.jewishvirtuallibrary.org/jsource/History/Kingdoms1.html.

69 Bing.com. (2015). "Bing Maps." Retrieved December, 4, 2015.

70 Bert Thompson, P. D. "Biblical Accuracy and Circumcision on the 8th Day." Retrieved December 27, 2015, from http://www.apologeticspress.org/APContent.aspx?category=13&article=1118.

71 Bing.com. (2015). "Bing Maps." Retrieved December, 4, 2015.

72 III, H. M. (2008). Exploring the Evidence for Creation. Eugene, Oregon, Harvest House.

73 Walter A., E., and Barry J. Beitzel. (1988). Baker Encyclopedia of the Bible.

[74] Elwell, W. A., & Beitzel, B. J. (1988). In *Baker encyclopedia of the Bible* (p. 629). Grand Rapids, MI: Baker Book House.

[75] Elwell, W. A., & Beitzel, B. J. (1988). In *Baker encyclopedia of the Bible* (p. 555). Grand Rapids, MI: Baker Book House.

[76] Kaufmann Kohler, J. L. M. (2016). "JewishEncyclopedia.com." Retrieved January 4, 2016, from http://jewishencyclopedia.com/articles/12012-pentecost.

[77] Powell, M. A. (2011). The HarperCollins Bible Dictionary (Revised and Updated). New York, HarperCollins.

[78] Tan-Gatue, P. (2015). The Lexham Bible Dictionary. J. D. Barry, Lexham Press.

[79] Thomas, R. L. (1998). New American Standard Hebrew-Aramaic and Greeek dictionaries.

[80] Chad, B. (2003). Holman Illustrated Bible Dictonary, Holman Bible Publishers.

[81] Elwell, W. A., & Beitzel, B. J. (1988). In *Baker encyclopedia of the Bible* (p. 1847). Grand Rapids, MI: Baker Book House.

[82] Elwell, W. A., & Beitzel, B. J. (1988). In *Baker encyclopedia of the Bible* (p. 1047). Grand Rapids, MI: Baker Book House.

[83] Walter A., E., and Barry J. Beitzel. (1988). Baker Encyclopedia of the Bible.

[84] Sharp, T. (2012). "How Big is Earth?" Retrieved December 26, 2015, from http://www.space.com/17638-how-big-is-earth.html.

[85] Slick, M. (2015). "Covenant." Retrieved August 8, 2015, from https://carm.org/christianity/christian-doctrine/covenant.

[86] Richards, L., & Richards, L. O. (1987). The teacher's commentary. Includes index. Wheaton, Ill, Victor Books.